BENEATH SAFER SKIES

A Child Evacuee in Shropshire

ANTHEA TOFT

MERLIN UNWIN BOOKS

First published by Merlin Unwin Books, 2014
Text © Anthea Toft 2014

Merlin Unwin Books Limited
Palmers' House, 7 Corve Street,
Ludlow, Shropshire, SY8 1DB
www.merlinunwin.co.uk

A CIP record of this book is available
from the British Library.
Printed and bound by TJ International, Padstow, England

ISBN 978-1-906122-65-2

Introduction

This story is based on over seventy letters written by my mother
to my father and on my own memories of when I was evacu-
ated. When war was declared and the Battle of Britain was
raging over our home in Kent, I was taken by my mother to live
in a remote valley on a working sheep farm on the borders of
Wales. My mother's anxiety, torn between fears for the safety
of her only child and love for her husband, led to our sudden
flight. She wrote to my father frequently describing our life
there. The letters seem very naive by today's standards but we
were without the knowledge that today's television coverage
can bring, and the bulletins of war news, listened to every day,
only added to our anxiety.

Communication with my father, left behind in Kent,
was restricted, as of course mobile phones were not yet in
use. Travel was difficult with petrol strictly rationed and all
sign posts and place names on railway stations removed. Any
journey to see us was long and arduous. Worry over my father
and the rest of the family left in the south was increased by the
mounting war news. Missing them, I often cried myself to sleep.
Every day brought fresh anxieties, with tales of bombing in all

the major cities and a growing fear of invasion. My mother's idea of planning for this event seems naive in the extreme. Our home village in Kent was designated as the last stand before the onslaught on London itself and my father's letters were full of news of the village being crowded with soldiers, guns and barbwire entanglements.

In the beautiful valley in which we found ourselves we were gradually assimilated into the farm life. It was a hard existence. Our first place, Mainstone Farm was rundown and dilapidated. It had no running water, no indoor sanitation, no electricity and very little heating. In the severe winter that followed I became ill and nearly died of pneumonia. In those days antibiotics and penicillin were not available and my mother resorted to kaolin poultices and my father to prayer. Deep snow prevented the doctor, on horseback, from reaching me.

Living in other people's houses was not easy. I had to learn to fit in with other ways and share other children's toys, since mine, with everything else, had been left behind. These experiences have affected me, I believe, all my life. I always feel the need to please. The loss of anything of mine is still a major tragedy. The fear of leaving home, even for a holiday, for many years made me anxious and sometimes even ill.

Everything became better when we moved to the much bigger Reilth Farm where a lively family of seven children welcomed me into their lives. I became fascinated by everything I saw done on the farm. I learnt to ride; to collect the eggs; to help in the harvest fields; to watch as bread, butter and poultry were prepared for the weekly market to which we went in the pony and trap; and to join in all the fun and games of this noisy household.

My mother was happy here but her letters were still full of plans to go home, which we eventually did, not to our own home but to another farm in Kent, until at last we found a house of our own and spent the last few years of the war enduring the bombardment from bombs and "doodle bugs".

I was always to remember that time in Shropshire. Eventually, after training as a teacher, I came back to work at a school for blind children and then to start up, with my husband, a group home for children with special needs, on a small holding not far from that beautiful valley. My great love of the countryside has been a lifelong passion. Nurtured as it was by my early years on a farm it has led to the writing of several books of poems and stories. Now looking back I feel that I owe much to my experiences in that wonderful valley.

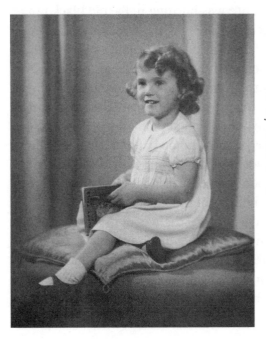

In Kent, aged four, and blissfully unaware of the great upheaval that was just about to overtake me

Chapter One

FARM LIFE
Early Summer 1940

The farmhouse kitchen was small and dark and, in spite of the July weather outside, a fire was burning in the old black range. Crouched on her knees in front of the fire, a small, white-haired woman held a cloth in one hand and a bar of strong-smelling soap in the other. In a large, studded, black leather chair, shabby and worn from long use, a big bulky man sat, sleeves rolled up, his black waistcoat unbuttoned, his feet in a basin of water. Slowly the woman bathed his feet with her worn red hands, while he sat, slumped and exhausted, staring into the fire. Just outside the door a wall-eyed collie lay on the damp flagstones. He too seemed worn out and we had to step over him to reach the interior of the kitchen.

As she heard our arrival, the woman straightened up, pushing her white hair aside with a damp hand.

'There you are then,' she said. 'Come along in. Mr Pugh is expecting you.'

I don't remember the long journey from Kent to Shropshire; the difficulties of travel in war-torn England, without signposts or road names, when reading a map made you an object of suspicion. The last few miles had been through trees down a narrow valley.

When we arrived there seemed nothing there, no friendly village street, only a few scattered houses, farm buildings, and then this house, small and square, half hidden by an enormous monkey-puzzle tree which grew so close to the building that its branches brushed against the small square windows. I don't remember leaving my home, my beloved father, my grannie and grandpa and most of my toys, to travel across England, almost into Wales, to this unknown place.

As I stood with my mother by the door it looked strange and alien, quite unlike the pleasant home I had lived in for the first seven years of my life. The kitchen in which we found ourselves had a grey stone-flagged floor. A huge Welsh dresser filled one wall, while at the far end stood the old black range. In the centre of the room was a rexine-covered table on which stood a large, flower-patterned teapot, brown-stained and chipped, and cups and saucers which looked thick and ugly compared to the fine china used for the dainty teas, served on a trolley with a silver teapot, with which my mother entertained her friends.

The man bent to put on his boots. He struggled to his feet to make us welcome. The woman hurried away with the bowl and went to swing the kettle on its bar over the fire. Pushing off the sleeping cats, Mr Pugh made room for us on the settle by the fire which smelt strongly of wood smoke and made my nose wrinkle. He asked us kindly about our journey, reassuring us in his soft lilting voice that we were most welcome.

Mr Pugh lived with his housekeeper Miss Ellige. They had been prepared to take in evacuees, as everyone with room to spare had been told to do, but were only too happy when they were asked by my great aunt Julia, who lived with Miss Chopping the school mistress of Mainstone, Shropshire, if they would take my mother and me as paying guests. I expect we were a slightly better bet than complete strangers and would, moreover, make some contribution to their already dwindling bank balance. I was living in Kent with my mother and father when the war started.

At first everything seemed much as usual, but as the news grew more and more alarming people began to realize the dangers of living in southern England so near to London. Many children were being sent away for safety. My cousins were booked on a boat to go to America but cancelled at the last minute when a boatload of children was torpedoed. My mother and her sister wondered what to do. Then my great aunt wrote from the wilds of Shropshire inviting them to bring their children to her. She only had room for one family but she promised to find rooms for my mother and me nearby. Advised by many to go while they still could, driven by the fear of harm to their children, many mothers left their husbands in the south-east and went, believing then that it would only be for a few short weeks.

My mother and I found ourselves on this small farm owned by Mr Pugh. The farmhouse was a poor place, draughty and damp. The stone floors were cold and the doors and windows ill-fitting. We had one small bedroom and shared the rest of the house with Mr Pugh and Miss Ellige. Luckily Mr Pugh loved children. He was big and gentle and made a large, secure friend for me. I grew to love sitting on his bulky lap while he snoozed in front of the fire and told me stories of his Welsh homeland. 'Tootie' he called me, which I found meant 'Little Dear'.

I came to follow him everywhere as, with his sheepdog,

he went about the farm. His manner was slow and forgetful and I know now that his bad management led to his downfall, but to me he was always kind and loving and I followed him like a shadow, deprived as I was of all but one of the familiar, much-loved adults in my earlier life.

Miss Ellige, on the other hand, was small, sharp and bitter-tongued. She was Mr Pugh's devoted slave. She resented our intrusion into her home and resented also the attention I received. She tried to be kind, but I felt, with a child's intuition, that she disliked me. Miss Ellige was 'chapel' and on the Sabbath, after attending the square chapel building in the opposite direction to the little church which my mother and I were sometimes to attend, she sat in the cold, unwelcoming sitting room, unused in the week when we all lived in the kitchen, reading her bible.

We had not been there long when, looking at me over the top of her steel pince-nez, she informed me that I was not to play with my toys on the Lord's day of rest. When my mother

The little chapel at Mainstone, Miss Ellige's preferred place of worship

11

protested, she agreed that I might read a book quietly. After we had been there some time we had further proof of her religious beliefs. One day Mr Pugh harnessed up the old horse and we all climbed into the trap to travel twenty miles to a farm near Welshpool to visit Miss Ellige's family. We were made welcome and given tea but I could not understand a word they said as they spoke only Welsh. To keep me amused I was put to sit opposite a huge picture which hung on the wall in the sitting room. It depicted, in great detail, the narrow way leading to Paradise and the broad way leading to destruction. The vision of hellfire was very vivid and I sat there a very long time. This impressed me enormously. I have never forgotten it.

On our first evening at the farm, the washing things were quickly put away and after tea we were invited to sit by

With Miss Ellige, learning the art of bottle-feeding lambs

the fire to recover after our long journey. But exhausted as they were after a day on the farm, our hosts were relieved when my mother said she would like to take me straight to bed. We were shown up some dark uncarpeted stairs to a small bedroom filled by a huge double bed. Its big goose-feather filled pillows and white cotton bedspread looked enormously inviting, and after a quick wash with cold water in the basin on the marble washstand, and a short prayer of thanks for our safe arrival and for the safety of my father left alone in Kent, I jumped into bed. The dark shadows caused by the flickering candle as it wavered in the draughts and the scratching of the monkey-puzzle tree against the window did not stop me from falling quickly asleep.

The next day things on the farm went on as usual. The work was hard. The buildings were neglected and tumbled-down, the yard covered in weed and thick dung, the animals thin and unhealthy. But to me it represented freedom. I spent hours in the fields at harvest-time watching Brownie, the old horse, drag the binder round and round or riding behind him on the heavy dray. The corn was full of thistles and my arms were scratched and sore as I struggled to pile the sheaves into stooks to help old John, the labourer, whose slow movements still seemed so much quicker than mine.

Old John wore faded blue clothes and a cloth cap. He kept a bottle of methylated spirits hidden in the hedge to refresh himself on the way round. He worked tirelessly whatever the weather but I believe he was often found drunk in a ditch somewhere and slept rough in one of the buildings. On those days in the fields however, as he struggled to save the poor crop while the rabbits played hide and seek in the corn, he was gentle and soft-spoken and very patient with my efforts. I remember him with great affection.

Old John worked tirelessly to save the poor crop while rabbits played hide-and-seek in the corn

A few cows were milked in the old cowshed. Fetched in each day from their thistle-filled field, they stood in the shadowy darkness of the old building munching gently and shifting their weight from one foot to the other on the cobbled floor. Mr Pugh milked them by hand, his bulky figure balanced precariously on a three-legged stool, as he murmured softly to them to yield up their milk. I shall always remember watching them from the open doorway with the rays of sunlight making

14

patterns on the cobbled floor. It was the first of many memories of shadowy cowsheds filled with the sweet smell of these my favourite animals. It was a distinct smell: their warm, grass-filled breath as I leaned over to fasten the chains round their velvety, wrinkled necks. Their soft friendly eyes would gaze at me placidly, their tails swishing as they stood patiently, pestered by flies, waiting to give up their meagre supply of milk. It was my treat to be given milk in a battered old mug straight from their soft warm teats. It was frothy and delicious and no doubt very unhygienic.

There were sheep on the farm, up on the high fields near Offa's Dyke. Many of them had patches of worms under their tails and were very thin. Some had that dreadful disease that made them turn in circles until they died. Sasnass was an orphan lamb that had to be fed each day from a bottle. His mother had died and no other sheep could be persuaded to take him. His wool was surprisingly hard and wiry, not soft as I had expected. His legs stuck out like sticks as I carried him about in my arms. I watched fascinated as Miss Ellige prepared his feed in an old wine bottle with a baby's teat on the end. It was warmed and cleaned with water out of the old black kettle on the range and then half filled with warm milk. I was allowed to hold it while he sucked fiercely at the teat, often covering both of us with the milk in his eagerness to get it all. I had to hold the bottle high to prevent air getting in and, as Sasnass grew very rough as he grew bigger, I had to hang on with both hands to prevent him butting it out of my grasp.

My only enemies were the geese. These large white birds inhabited the field close to the house and were often hanging about the back door. From the moment they came hissing from their shed to guzzle voraciously at their trough of meal and kitchen scraps, they kept a beady eye on all who went in and out and were as keen as watchdogs to warn of the approach of any stranger. They would then rush at them with their heads close to the ground and wings outstretched, hissing fiercely. They could give a good peck and, I was told, could break my arm with their wings. I kept well clear. The geese had a daily routine that hardly varied. They would take themselves off to the stream for a swim, led by the gander, at about the same time each day. On the bank the ground was covered with feathers where they had preened themselves. This task was often concluded with a triumphant cackle when, standing on tiptoe, they would raise their beaks high in the air and compete with each other in making the most noise. The only time I had cause to be grateful to them was when, leaning on the rickety fence by the back door and chatting to Miss Ellige who was pounding dough in the kitchen, the fence broke and I fell backwards onto the cobbles below. A lump as big as an egg came up on the back of my head and, to comfort me, Miss Ellige gave me a large white goose egg. This I sold to my aunt for sixpence.

The days passed and I grew used to living there. Letters from my father told of bombing raids over London: of the Battle of Britain being waged over his head, of the terrible struggle taking place to repel the German bombers and of the preparations for the invasion of England that Hitler promised was soon to take place. In August Winston Churchill gave his famous speech praising our airmen with the words, 'Never .... was so much owed by so many to so few'. But the news grew worse and Churchill warned parliament that invasion could be any day. 'Perhaps tonight, perhaps next week, perhaps never,' were his words. Hitler actually named the day of the invasion, first as the seventh and then as the fifteenth of September. Huge masses of landing barges were gathered in the French ports and massed troops were poised waiting for the command to invade, but perhaps because of the relentless bombing by our forces, he seemed to change his mind and it was postponed again. News came from Romania of atrocities and a terrible earthquake there. Nearer home, as we looked up into the quiet skies over the Mainstone valley, came the news of the terrible bombing of our major cities.

As time went by and winter approached, my aunt and cousins and some friends who had come with us to Shropshire became unhappy and restless and spoke of returning home. My mother was torn between her loyalty to her husband and the safety of her only child. The separation from my father was made worse by our lack of contact. Apart from his letters, often accompanied by little packets of sweets, we heard little of him, as phone calls were very difficult. The only call box

My father, Leslie Constable, nicknamed Johnnie

My mother, Dorothy Constable, nicknamed Tommie

was a quarter of a mile away down the lane and there was often a four-hour delay to be connected.

Life in the farmhouse was hard and often dreary. We had no electricity or running water. The house was very cold and we began to run short of fuel. I began to show signs of the asthma and bronchitis that was to make me ill all through my early years. Because of the dangers to our merchant ships, which were being attacked by German U-boats with devastating effect, there were many shortages. Rationing began to bite. Bananas were unknown. Coming from the 'Garden of England' as we did, we found the food rather stodgy and the shortage of fresh fruit and vegetables very trying. But compared to others, we were extremely lucky.

We heard dreadful stories of the bombing of London. Many people were homeless. Some were said to be camping out in the Kentish hop fields or in Epping Forest. Some had made a temporary home in the caves at Chislehurst in Kent. London was burning. Every effort was being made to stop the bombers reaching the city. This meant that they were often turned back over my home in Kent where they would jettison their bomb load before returning home. The area round my grandparents house in Sussex was declared a defence area and cleared of visitors and children. Piers were blown up, hotels requisitioned and sandbagged gun emplacements sprang up everywhere. The ten-mile stretch round Brighton had 3,000 men to protect it. Hearing all this and frightened to return home my mother grew more resigned to a long stay. Homesick and worried as she was, she was thankful to have this haven, however uncomfortable it might be, where we could wait for better times. Standing under the quiet, starry skies of Shropshire, we prayed that my father would be safe.

Chapter Two

THE TIME BEFORE

Autumn 1939

On the Sunday afternoon that war was declared my mother and father and I were in the sitting room of our house Little Harcourt in Pembury, Kent. I was making fruit out of plasticine and our dog Monty was watching me. It was a pretty house of warm red brick and leaded windows. The Virginia creeper which clung to the walls was turning red and butterflies hovered over the Michaelmas daisies which filled the herbaceous borders flanking the path leading to the sundial. Beyond the old orchard, where my swing hung, and beyond a privet hedge, was the vegetable garden where Mr Malthouse grew his vegetables for us to enjoy. Lately, my father had had a dugout shelter made near the raspberries but it had become filled with water and a few frogs. No one really thought we would find a use for it.

My parents had moved to this house from a smaller one in Romford Road, Pembury when I was four. It was about three and a half miles from where my father worked in a bank in Tunbridge Wells. Pembury was a pleasant village in those days, surrounded by the beautiful countryside of the Kent and Sussex border. This was the so-called Garden of England, full of apple orchards, hop fields and pretty villages of red-tiled houses, often grouped round a village green or a pond where ducks swam. Such a safe, secure world it seemed then. Our lives were fairly uneventful. Each day my father went to work at 'the office'.

He had planned his life differently when, as a young man, he hoped to be an architect, but at the end of the First World War when he was invalided out of hospital, he was glad to be offered a job in his uncle's bank. This work never suited him very well. His health was not good and much of his working life was spent in a small dark office lit only by electric light. He was a gentle, sensitive man who, although he had wanted a son to carry on the family name, had soon learnt to love his little

daughter and spent many hours playing with me and making things for me.

My mother was a careful housewife. The house was always charming and well kept, filled with sunlight and

Happy times for mother and father in Pembury, 1938

flowers. The sitting room had low windows looking out onto the lawns and flowerbeds and chintz covers on the furniture. Taking up a great part of it was the Bechstein grand piano which had been given to my father by his uncle, Harry Gates, and which was his pride and joy. Music was my father's great love. He came from a family of musicians and church organists on his mother's side, tracing back to Bernard Gates, master of the choristers at Westminster Abbey and a friend of Handel.

He had learnt to play both the piano and organ extremely well. In those last days of peace as the war clouds gathered, friends would come to enjoy music together and I would go to sleep listening to Chopin, Liszt, and Schumann. My mother would sing songs such as 'A little Brown Bird Singing' or 'I'll Walk Beside You' or Roger Quilter's 'Now Sleeps the Crimson Petal'. There were snatches from 'Merrie England' or tunes from Gilbert and Sullivan and often the sound of lively duets, accompanied by loud instructions, played by my father and Jens Boysen.

Jens had come as a student to England from his native Germany to lodge in the house opposite us where he married the eldest daughter, Mollie, and they had a small girl named Lorna. My father and he spent many happy hours together, but as war approached, he came to bid us a sad goodbye before returning to Germany to fight on the 'other side'. Mollie and Lorna went with him and spent much of the war hiding in their cellar in Aachen. It was many years later that he returned to England and he and my father were able to resume their friendship and play duets together again.

In those days most middle-class families had servants. Although we were not particularly well-off we had a succession of maids who wore a smart black uniform with a frilly white cap and apron for the afternoon when they opened the door to friends as they called for tea. My mother had a little bell which she would ring for the tea trolley to be brought in. There were sugar tongs, a silver teapot and fine bone china, and always a sponge cake and thinly-cut sandwiches. My mother welcomed her visitors with dignity except when her dog, Monty, bit one of them as she came to the door.

One person who seemed to be always with us was Mr Malthouse's daughter Mrs Churchill. In the mornings she did the cooking but in the afternoons she devoted herself to looking after me. She was a strong, big-boned woman who wore her black hair in 'earphones'. She had a direct no-nonsense manner and, with brown eyes sparkling behind gold-rimmed glasses, did not hesitate to tell my mother what she thought, nor me how to behave. But her fierceness belied a heart of gold and we were devoted to each other.

Little Harcourt where we were living when war was declared in 1939

Some of my earliest memories are of our rambles through the countryside when she would drag my old pushchair, both of us laughing and happy, down the Kentish lanes filling it with branches, flowers and moss; and the times when I played about while she picked hops on a neighbouring farm.

Often at weekends we would go to Lewes in Sussex where both my mother and father were born, to visit my grandparents. My mother had been born in a tall house, hung with grey slates, over my grandfather's jewellery shop by the bridge over the River Ouse. My father had lived in an equally tall slate-covered house within a few hundred yards, just across the river.

By the time I knew them my grandparents were living in a beautiful Victorian house, under the Downs on the Kingston Road, which they had re-named 'Glengariff'. It had a large garden, a tennis court, orchards, outhouses and stables and to me it was paradise. I loved my grandmother dearly and, I think because I resembled a child she had lost at the age of three, I was the favourite and adored grandchild. I remember the comfort of being allowed to creep into her bed in the morning where she lay, in a large white nightdress, her beautiful white hair spread on the pillow, and told me stories of her childhood with her seven brothers and sisters. I remember watching as she made huge apple pies on the scrubbed kitchen table or managed to cook a meal for all of us on the kitchen range and oil stoves in the scullery. I remember the feel of the soft fur of her large black collar as I snuggled against her while Uncle Bert, my grandfather's brother, preached his long pulpit-thumping sermons in the Tabernacle each Sunday, where my uncle Leslie played the organ, perched high above us in the gallery.

I remember the peaceful evenings while she sat reading, a bag of sweets and a glass of water by her side, while her gold

Hop picking in Kent just before the war

pince-nez gradually slipped down her beautiful aquiline nose (of which she was very proud). I remember her sitting regally upright under an awning on the lawn, pouring tea, while the family lounged in deck-chairs, swung in the hammock or played croquet.

My grandfather had a stuffed canary under a glass dome in his study and when I was very quiet he would take off the dome and let me stroke it. Then I would get a ride in his swivel chair before being told to leave him in peace. When I knew him he spent most of his time in the garden. My great-grandfather had divided his estate between three of his four sons on which they were to set up their respective homes.

My grandfather remained in the original house. The garden was wonderful. Long grass paths led between herbaceous borders, turning sudden corners into secret places which invited exploration. Apples and plums lay in profusion under the orchard trees. Flowers could be picked in huge bunches:

daffodils, narcissi, polyanthus and violets were given to us, tied up with care by my grandfather in the potting shed where a huge swathe of raffia hung for that purpose. Vegetables filled our car as we went home: marrows, carrots, beans and potatoes: and pots of jam made by my grandmother, of quince jelly, rhubarb and ginger, plum and apricot. In the apple shed, where special wooden shelves were loaded with many named varieties of apples, there was a wonderful smell. My grandfather heaped baskets with Cox's Orange Pippins, Bramley Seedling and Russets to see us through the winter. How much we were going to miss all this when we were far away in Shropshire. This dear old place was the centre of our family life and that of my dear grandparents who were to wait anxiously for our return. The whole place was full of memories of my mother's childhood with her sister Kathleen, her brother Wilfred and their many cousins.

On the side of the house leading out of the dining room was a conservatory with red quarry-tile paths and white shelving. Geraniums filled it with their strange scent and a beautiful white rose was trained above our heads. My cousin and I had an old wind-up gramophone and we would dress

Glengarrif, my grandparents' home outside Lewes, Sussex – a place of endless happiness for me

25

My grandparents, Winifred and Walter Kenward on their Golden Wedding day

up and dance among the flowers, dreaming of the dances which my mother and her sister were so fond of discussing, and wearing their cast-off Edwardian dresses with fringes and sequins, fans and headdresses which were our delight. Beyond the garden stretched the Downs; beautiful and serene, where the cloud shadows raced.

From my little bedroom above the front door, across the flat water-meadows we called 'The Brooks' I could see Mount Caburn and Firle Beacon on either side of the Eastbourne Gap. I loved this view and would often go to sleep with my head on the window ledge listening to the late birdcalls from the dark garden below me. It seemed as if it would go on for ever...

I think it dawned on people slowly that the war might affect them. The first real intimation that it might, after the shock of the first pronouncement and the noise of the siren that followed, was, for us, the sudden pile of gas masks in our dining room, all in their brown cardboard boxes.

We had just been given a Jewish refugee from Austria to look after – a little girl who had seen her grandparents murdered in their own garden. She could not speak many words of English and my father propped a dictionary against the teapot as we tried to speak to her. She seemed to me to need a lot of attention from him, sitting on his knee, and I hated her for it. When she saw the gas masks she screamed and cried out, 'The Germans will come. They will kill you all.' I think it frightened me. I was too young to understand. We quarrelled and I banged her head on the cupboard and she scratched my arm.

My parents began to listen to the news every day with grim faces. In the brilliant, cloudless spring weather of early 1940 we waited. By the 28 May the evacuation of Dunkirk was already taking place. France capitulated. The news of the German advance through Europe was terrifying. Denmark,

On the swings at Pembury recreational ground

Norway, Holland, Belgium, Luxemburg and France had fallen to the Panzers in two short months. It was difficult to know in detail what was happening. Censorship was strict. We listened to Lord Haw-Haw's bulletins from Hamburg.

At home evacuation had begun and everyone spoke of the safety of the children. My cousins were booked on a ship for America but their parents cancelled it at the last minute when they heard of a terrible tragedy involving the loss of a ship carrying hundreds of children. My father joined the A.R.P. and was in charge of distributing gas masks and seeing that the blackout was enforced. Ration books were issued and petrol rationing began. It was a beautiful summer but barbed wire fences clogged the beaches and a ten-mile restriction from the coast meant that we had to have a permit to visit my grandparents in Lewes. All street names and signposts were removed and the church bells were silenced, to be used only as a signal of invasion. Gradually the terrible possibilities were realized. In the summer of 1940 a second evacuation of children took place. My grandmother's eldest sister, who lived in the remote village of Mainstone in Shropshire, wrote inviting my mother and her sister to bring their children to her where she would find them accommodation until things settled down.

Leaving my father and our home, to which we were never to return, we left for Shropshire.

Chapter Three

IDYLLIC SUMMER TURNS TO WINTER

Summer 1940

The Shropshire valley in which we found ourselves became our new world. Separated from our family in Kent and all we had left behind we learnt to adapt to our new surroundings where, for much of the time, my mother and I were left to our own devices until the normal life of this community, which had found its own patterns of survival over many years, gradually absorbed us.

Here in Mainstone the days passed in relative peace and safety. Our lives settled into some sort of normality. It must have been a worrying and lonely time for my mother, 'a stranger in a strange land'; but we soon fell into a routine, taking an interest in the farm life, exploring the countryside and writing many letters home to my father. My mother's sister with her two children, Robin and Margaret, and Ruth (a friend from the Pembury days) with her twin boys, Peter and Paul, were also boarding nearby and we were some company for one another; but mostly we were on our own.

My mother had always enjoyed country life and this helped her to pass the time more happily. Thrown together for company we took an almost equally childlike delight in our daily walks together, watching the changes as summer turned into autumn, and our new home grew familiar and became loved. Sometimes I was joined by other children as I played in the long days of late summer. I had a child's ability to live in the present and leave the dark shadows which hung over us to the nights when, hearing the dread sound of enemy bombers going over us in wave after wave on their mission of destruction to the cities, I cried with homesickness and for my father.

A stream ran through the valley; past the farms where ducks and geese muddied its clear waters; past the school whose playground merged into the fields. On its banks the children played endless games, caught tiddlers in jam jars or tried to dam its fast current with stones, mud and sticks which were quickly washed away.

Below the school the stream flowed under a little bridge. Its railings were just the right height for leaning on, for turning somersaults over, for watching the water flowing so swiftly past us that it made us giddy as we played 'Pooh sticks' with bits of twig torn from the hedges. In places in the valley the stream flowed peacefully through flat water meadows, serene and beautiful, where cattle grazed quietly and swallows darted overhead. It flowed over pebbles, brown and golden. It sparkled and glinted in the sunshine. The water was very cold and very clear although we were told not to drink it.

On its brink were water plants, cuckoo pint and kingcups and reeds which hid the nests of moorhen and coot, and the holes of vole and water rat. In places where the ground

Playing with Peter and Paul, the Garrett twins, in the stream in the Mainstone valley

was flat the cattle came down to drink and the soft mud was churned into water-filled hoof prints which paled as they baked hard in the sun. On the banks little beaches had formed of round pebbles where we played and paddled and explored the tree roots laid bare by erosion. Willow and elder hung over the stream and in the dark places gnats gathered. Twisted into strange shapes the roots became anything our imagination required, forming those secret dens which are so much a part of a country child's memories.

These were magical places where, with bare toes and dresses tucked into our knickers, we were drawn into a closeness with the natural world of water, plants, air and sunlight that only children know how to enter.

31

*The church of
St John the
Baptist at
Mainstone*

On either side of the valley woods rose steeply, shutting us in to this quiet world, enclosing the valley as though shielding it from harm, as indeed they did shield it from the worst of the winds, which swept over the high hills. Through these woods rutted cart tracks led up to the high pastures. Overhung by tall untrimmed hedges, they were shady and cool on warm days. In damp places where trickles of water came out of the rocky banks, ferns grew and moss covered the stones. Along the tops of the banks, bracken and whinberries flourished and blackberries overhung the walls. In the woody areas were the red caps of fly agaric which, seen by me for the first time, looked like fairy villages.

The hedges were tall and wild and full of life. Birds nests were hidden among their branches and butterflies and moths enjoyed the damp grass on their banks. In autumn they glowed with the red berries of rowan, hawthorn and holly. Hazelnuts grew in clusters among their golden leaves and sloes and elderberries waited to be gathered. Above the woods the hills were bare. Open to the winds, their turf nibbled short by the sheep, the trees bent by the wind, they were a place of cloud shadows and silence. Right on the border between England and Wales, Offa's Dyke spanned the hills; a shallow ditch where the sheep lay out of the wind and where we played and picnicked on sunny days.

That autumn in 1940, while the war clouds gathered momentum, we watched the harvest being gathered into the old stone barns, helping where we could in the fields. In the little stone church we sang the harvest hymns with gratitude more heartfelt than usual for the bounties of the countryside. The fields were bare now and the short stubble gave us a freedom to walk where we pleased while the rabbits ran before us and the sun cast long shadows and turned everything to gold. Along the lanes the hedgerow fruits were ripening and as we walked, often joined by my cousins and other children, we filled our baskets with anything that pleased us. We gathered blackberries, staining our fingers and scratching our legs on the trailing briars. Hazelnuts were still soft enough to break between our teeth. Trailing vines of bryony, bright as red jewels, wound among the branches, but these we avoided as they were poisonous to humans. We found sweet chestnuts falling from their spiky cases and took them back to be boiled or roasted on the bars of the old black grate of the kitchen range.

A great tree of conkers grew near the school and I collected the shiny brown fruit, especially the ones with flat surfaces, to make into dolls' furniture or to put on a string for a game of conkers. Acorn cups and beech mast cases were made into brooches and button holes. Dried grasses were woven into mats or little round baskets. Collections of leaves were pressed between blotting paper to try to retain their glorious colours or scribbled over to make patterns and silhouettes to be labelled, coloured and admired later by the fire. A few last foxgloves bent over the lanes and we fitted their cool flowers over our fingers. The sticky hooks of the burdock which clung to our jumpers were named 'sweethearts' and caused much light-hearted teasing. There was endless entertainment to be had when there was nothing else to do.

In September I started school and began to make friends with some of the children in the neighbourhood. This left my mother even more alone and her letters to my father were rather unhappy. As winter drew on our life became more difficult. Bad weather kept us indoors and the cold, damp house began to take its toll. Everyone seemed to have constant colds and I was often laid up with bronchitis and asthma.

When I was well enough I struggled along the muddy lanes to school. Dressed in welly boots, mackintosh and sou'wester even so I was often soaked by the time I reached there. We were practising carols for Christmas. The haunting tune of 'In the bleak midwinter' still reminds me of that little classroom on a winter's afternoon, with the sweet sound drifting out across the valley while the snow began to fall.

1940 was the worst winter on record since 1895 and the valley filled with snow many feet deep. Struggling to keep their livestock fed, the farmers were exhausted. The roads were quickly blocked and no one came into the village except for the postman or an occasional horse and cart with essential provisions from the town of Bishop's Castle four and a half miles away.

Most farmers had managed to clear their high fields of sheep before the snow came and the fields close to the farms were crowded. The sheep were hardy and self-sufficient. They used their hooves to scrape away the snow, but the sparse grass was not enough and it was heavy and exhausting work dragging hay and water out to them where they huddled in the lee of a wall. There were stories of sheep trapped under

The winter of 1940 was the most severe on record and at Mainstone the snow lay deep on the lane

the snow which had to be dug out; of how one man's dog had found ten sheep huddled by a wall, all dead and another who found his stock still alive thanks to the tireless efforts of his sheepdog. Animals everywhere were threatened with starvation and the farmers worked endlessly to save them. A few were left to fend for themselves. After trying in vain to get a bale of hay, we watched helplessly as the pony in the field behind the school grew weaker until, floundering in the deep drifts trying to reach water, it fell one night and died in the stream.

Of course the winter weather was very beautiful. The air was clear and the sun shone on the expanses of white which covered everything. The wind had blown the snow into great drifts many feet deep and it was possible to walk over the five-bar gates into the fields. Narrow pathways had been dug along some of the lanes but these were often filled again overnight by a fresh snowfall. The silence was intense. Icicles formed and the trees, covered by a glistening layer of frost, gave off tiny tinkling sounds as their frozen twigs brushed against each other. Wild animal life took advantage of the hidden paths under the hedgerows and, except for the rabbits, were seldom seen. We were marooned, lost in a world that was forced to be almost completely self-sufficient. News from the outside world grew steadily more frightening.

We heard of the bombing of Coventry, of Birmingham, Sheffield, Manchester, Portsmouth, Bristol, Southampton and Liverpool. Horrific stories, that seemed almost unreal in our sheltered valley, came to us over the crackling airwaves. Night after night London was the prime target. In the beautiful moonlit nights this meant that, night after night, planes were flying over my home in Kent. The skies were alight with the flames of incendiary bombs and my father was busy fire-watching. Losses on both sides were mounting. Dog-fights raged over the Kentish countryside. Our neighbour's son who was a fighter pilot was killed at the age of 21. The Kent airfield of Biggin Hill was attacked. All this meant that Pembury was very much in the thick of things. There were forty large guns in that village alone.

We lived in fear of the bad news that each day brought. My father wrote of Pembury being full of soldiers and bombs falling in our old road. He said the light of the fires in London were visible each night as he did his fire duty. Grannie sent us some apples from the garden and told us she was making Christmas puddings, but still thought it would be wrong for us to return home.

My mother wrote to my father about our belongings

which had been hurriedly stored and which might be spoiling, and of the things we would need if we stayed on through the winter. As she sat listening to the news, read by the familiar voice of Alvar Lidell or Stuart Hibberd, my mother's face conveyed the seriousness of my father's position to me, and I lay awake worrying that I would never see him again. The coming of Mr Rosser, the postman, was looked for eagerly every day. We longed for every scrap of news from home and gave him in return letters for my father and my grandparents. That winter Mr Rosser was often our only connection with the world outside our valley. He would walk over the hills to the remote farmsteads, about twenty miles a day in all weathers. He would bring us news from further up the valley as he sat and thawed out and drank his tea. Sometimes he was offered something stronger and, on one occasion, he was found drunk in a ditch with his letters scattered around him. Poor man! His reputation suffered but his courage and perseverance were much appreciated in that dreary time.

There seems to be a curious blank in my memory of Christmas that year. I remember practising carols in school, but after that, nothing. Did I get any presents, any cards, any Christmas dinner? I suppose so. Where were we on the day that Christ was born? The dark world seems to have blotted it all out. The memories too painful perhaps. Broken promises of being home for Christmas, too difficult to handle. The previous year, every detail remembered; the family, the tree, Father Christmas coming up the long drive to the house, lights, music, my grandmother serenely cooking for 21 of us. I can even remember the books I was given in their lovely white shiny wrappers. This year – blank – nothing, not one happy memory. It was a long winter which grew more difficult as time went on.

Chapter Four

CRISIS

Winter 1940

It was one day in December that something happened at school that made me really ill. It was a bitter day of ice and fog. I was with a group of bigger girls on the far side of the stream when the bell was rung for the end of playtime. Glad for once to be allowed back inside, we turned to cross the stream. Most of the girls were big enough to jump it easily but I hesitated. 'Come on,' they cried. 'It's easy.' One of them quickly seized me to help me across. Just as she leapt, a stone tilted, and losing her balance, she dropped me into the icy water. I was rushed indoors crying with shock and dripping wet. After a quick rub-down I was taken home to my mother for a change of clothes. By then, however, I had caught a chill and bronchitis quickly turned to pneumonia.

In those days, before penicillin was widely used, pneumonia was a serious illness which reached a climax when one either began to recover or died. I had already had this illness when I was five and had been very ill for five months. My mother was desperately worried. She sat by me in the big bed as I lay drifting in and out of consciousness, staring at the huge monkey-puzzle tree outside our bedroom window and feeling very alone. Her sister, Kathleen, had returned home with her two children before the winter set in, and we had no one except my old aunt to turn to. The room was dark, lit only by an oil lamp standing on the washstand. Paper was peeling off the walls where patches of damp had loosened it. The window was so badly fitting that she had to stuff newspaper into the crevices to keep out the bitter draughts. Outside the lane was deserted and deep in snow. Occasionally, as my mother waited, she could hear movements from the kitchen below or the clank of a pail as water was drawn from the well. The only hot water was from the large kettle which hung over the kitchen range and she did not like to ask for this too often.

As my temperature rose, she wished desperately that the road was clear enough to get me to hospital or for a doctor to visit me. We heard from Mr Rosser that men had started to dig out the road towards Bishop's Castle, four and a half long miles away, and that a party from there was digging in our direction; but when they were within shouting distance the snow fell again and we were cut off once more. Mr Pugh, my devoted friend, was beside himself. He tiptoed round the house asking every few minutes how I

How many letters did we send from this box?

was, his big red face puckered in dismay. Miss Ellige made me bread and milk and gruel but I couldn't eat and lay tossing in delirium as the crisis approached. One can only guess at my mother's state of mind as my temperature continued to rise. I was weak and often delirious and my breathing became more and more laboured. Mr Pugh offered to try to fetch a doctor on horseback but more snow made it impossible to make the attempt. One night he helped my mother reach the phone box at the other end of the village. Delays of several hours were frequent owing to the devastation in the cities, where many lines were down, but eventually she spoke to my father, far away in Kent. He too felt helpless and desperately worried. He did the only thing he could think of. He phoned the 'White Sisters' in Dorset, a religious community which he and my mother had visited on holiday the previous year. It was a place of peace and love. Quelling his reservations, he asked the sisters to pray for me. That night they lit candles and kept up constant prayers for my recovery. Far away in Shropshire my mother watched at my bedside, waiting for the crisis she was sure would take place soon... It never came. My temperature abated and by the next morning I was beginning to recover. Soon I was sitting up in bed listening to the story of 'Mary Plain', which my father had sent to cheer me up. My mother had made up her mind, however. Kind as they were, Mr Pugh and Miss Ellige were struggling with their own problems.

It was time for us to make a move. I suppose moving was something that affected many wartime children. It was always a disturbing feature of my childhood. Whether my mother was particularly restless and anxious I don't know, but we frequently moved or made plans to move which were discussed in great detail in her letters to my father. I think this had a profound effect on me as a child; it certainly affected my schooling. Before the age of twelve I had attended six different schools and had been taught at home by several different people usually for a few short weeks. I think that it affected me in other ways too.

Outwardly a confident and friendly child, I had a deep sense of insecurity. My favourite imaginative game which I remember playing over and over again was to pack up all my toys in my pram and explain to them we were going on a long journey. I can still remember the sense of urgency that accompanied this game. I often could not bear to hear about a coming change and would run out of the room with my hands over my ears or would even develop asthma and a temperature which prevented us from going. Children who stayed at home in the bombed cities had of course a much worse time, but being moved around and always in other people's houses has, I believe, given me a lifelong fear of change and a feeling of always having to make an effort to fit in. When I was twelve, we settled down and I attended school regularly for the first time. I loved it – but that is another story.

Delays of several hours were frequent owing to the devastation in the cities

Chapter Five

END OF A HILL FARMER

Winter 1940

The war dragged on. U-boat attacks on our merchant ships in the Atlantic led to increasing food shortages and everyone was expected to tighten their belts. Rationing was strict. Points and coupons were needed for many essential things. There were more and more regulations and instructions issued by the government. The production of food became of utmost importance. People everywhere were told to dig up their lawns and flowerbeds to grow vegetables. Every scrap of kitchen waste was used for feeding chickens or a pig, while farmers were encouraged to make use of every available acre of land to grow food crops. They received subsidies for ploughing, fertilizing and for draining the land. That year, and for several years to come, everyone who could, worked in the fields to bring in the harvest.

Many women joined the Women's Land Army in preference to joining the forces, and in their khaki and green uniform, often brought fun and laughter to the heavy work. Prisoners too were used, and Conscientious Objectors could opt for work on the land. In Mainstone children were often missing from school when they were kept at home to help on the farm. Boys of thirteen or fourteen did the work of men. Even small children lent a hand. It was a hard struggle. By then farms were graded A B or C and those in the C group could be requisitioned and have their land taken from them.

Was it bad luck or bad judgement that, unlike other farms in the Mainstone valley, Mr Pugh's farm was so run-down? Some said he had the reputation of being a loser. It was certain that a run of bad luck brought him to final ruin. That autumn he and John, his farm worker, struggled hard to keep the farm going, but it was a losing battle. His machinery was old and often broke down. Brownie, his old horse, was expected to work without ceasing; every ounce of his strength went into pulling the binder and the heavily-laden cartloads of thistle-ridden corn back to the barn. Brownie was big, gentle and wise but the continual overwork undermined his health.

The end came when, exhausted from struggling in the snow to milk and feed the cows, Mr Pugh decided to leave the old horse in the top barn overnight instead of fetching him home. That night more snow fell and Brownie was trapped in the barn without food or water. Weakened by his unstinting efforts at harvest time he collapsed and died before help could reach him. We watched sadly as his heavy carcass was chained and dragged down through the snow – an undignified end for such a faithful creature. A great loss to any farmer, it was one of the blows which brought about the end of Mr Pugh's farming life.

The land was run-down and neglected; the buildings in disrepair. The fields were covered in thistles and encroached by bracken, their hedges in need of laying and their gates broken. Many of the sheep were infested with maggots or aborted their lambs. The cows gave a meagre supply of milk and their calves raised little at market. Extra food production seemed out of the question.

One day another blow fell which shocked everyone. Mr Pugh shot his own sheepdog. It was an accident which never should have happened. He had taken his gun out after supper to go rabbiting and, so he said, his dog disobeyed him and ran in front of his gun. It was an unforgivable offence for a sheep farmer who relied heavily on his dog to do the work among the sheep. It was the last straw. The local farmers were shocked but not surprised. They all knew the end was near and that Mainstone Farm would soon change hands. We were aware that things were badly wrong. We met Miss Ellige crying in the lane. She told us the farm was to go. They were leaving and going to live in Montgomery. My mother's mind was made up. We were moving to School House.

Chapter Six

AUNT JULIA
January 1941

When we arrived at School House, the kitchen was full of children. Some evacuees were sitting miserably at the table drinking mugs of cocoa and some local children, who had come to help, were making a lot of noise. Miss Chopping, the village schoolmistress, was waving a list in one hand while she tried to maintain order. I think my mother had expected some sort of welcome but Miss Chopping was not to be deterred from her job as billeting officer by the arrival of Aunt Julia's relatives. She merely waved us towards a door leading into the other part of the house, while she continued to survey the frightened faces of this latest batch of evacuees and ascertain their names before allocating them to their new homes.

The children seemed to be between five and ten. Clutching their few belongings, white-faced and dirty, they gazed at her, forlornly answering to their names in whispers. One small child, who was crying bitterly, clung to another as though fearing to be parted. My mother and I put down our luggage and went into the next room where we found Aunt Julia, knitting busily. Aunt Julia was my grandmother's eldest sister. She had the same lovely white hair, but hers was cut short and her face, with its sightless eyes, lacked the sweet expression of her sister. She turned as we entered, however, and held out a hand to make us welcome. Deterred by the sight of the first blind person I had seen at close quarters, I hung back, but my mother pushed me forward and, gritting my teeth, I bent to kiss her, trying not to think of the watery empty lids where her eyes should have been.

Aunt Julia was a person of very strong views. The eldest of eight children, all of whom were strong-willed and intelligent, she was, in the days when women were beginning to fight for their rights, determined to be independent and fight for the things she believed in. In her youth she had lived in London. After going to Girton College she became a suffragette and secretary to a socialist member of parliament. But suddenly, at the age of thirty, her life changed dramatically. She went blind. Now an old lady, she was living in Shropshire, where she shared a house and where the village schoolmistress, Miss Chopping, looked after her. It was she who had written to my mother and her sister Kathleen telling them to bring their children, my cousin Robin, six months older than myself, and his sister Margaret, three years younger, and me, away from the bombs to the comparative safety of Shropshire. My cousins were the first to live with Aunt Julia, while we were on the farm, but later they returned to the south. When Mr Pugh's farm was sold we moved into School House to share their home with the two maiden ladies.

We were given a light and airy room at the back of the house looking over the fields and up the valley of Cwmfrith.

This was our bedroom but as it had a fireplace, we were often able to sit up there when we wanted to be on our own. Mostly we lived downstairs sharing everything with the two ladies who had very definite views about how things should be done. It was a strict regime. My mother and I, used to gentler ways, found it difficult.

My aunt had strong opinions about most things and was very critical of the way I was being brought up. I was constantly reproved. My mother's nervousness about my health, made worse by her fear of losing me during my illness at the farm, was seen as over-indulgence. Aunt Julia was never ill herself, in fact she was so hardy that she would sleep by an open window with snow blowing in onto her bed. She did not understand my childish ailments. She thought my mother mollycoddled me, so she and Miss Chopping set about putting things right. Everything I did was criticised, especially if it seemed 'soft'. They thought I needed hardening off. When I was at school Miss Chopping would send me out to play without a coat in the bitter weather. I was often in bed with a raised temperature and a return of the bronchitis which made me cough but this weakness was ignored.

My mother resented all this deeply and became more and more unhappy. She was asked to help more in the house and complained bitterly in her letters to my father that too much was expected of her and she was treated like a servant. Most of the time though we all got along quite well. It could not have been easy for them having us at that time. Miss Chopping's job at the school was far from easy and shortages made house-keeping increasingly difficult.

Mealtimes were something of a nightmare for me, as my aunt's empty eye sockets would weep into her food and her table manners were inevitably clumsy. Meals were plain and good. I was told in no uncertain terms that, 'You eat to live, not live to eat'. Every morsel had to be cleared from our plates. This also applied to artichokes, which I hated. Of course they were quite right. Food had become very short. In 1941 merchant ships were being sunk at the rate of three a day. Rationing was strict. It was 'fair shares for everyone', but two ounces of butter per person a week, one ounce of cheese, one or two eggs and half a pint of milk did not go far. Children were given cod liver oil and orange juice to supplement their diet and mothers struggled to keep their families fed.

Many people tried to have a little extra by keeping chickens, rabbits or a pig. Vegetables were grown instead of flowers. Fruit was made into jam, for which one could get extra sugar, or bottled to keep for the winter. In the days before freezers were thought of, vegetables, such as beans, were stored in layers of salt. Eggs were preserved in isinglass. Some things were obtainable from 'under the counter' and every housewife tried to keep a store of food in case of emergency. In many of her letters to my father, my mother enquired anxiously about the stores she had left behind and suggested plans for him to grow extra vegetables in preparation for our return.

People were very conscious of how necessary it was to help the war effort by saving all they could. There were constant reminders from the government of ways we could all make our contribution. We were a besieged island, our merchant ships running terrible risks to bring us essential supplies. We were fighting for survival with everything in our power. Rallied on by Winston Churchill's resounding speeches we all felt called upon to do everything we could to help. Everything that could be salvaged was collected and sent for recycling to help the war effort; aluminium, rags, tins, bottles, laddered stockings, books for pulp and iron gates and railings. Petrol was rationed, also clothes and furniture. A supply of coupons was issued to each person to use when buying these things. Everyone made do with old clothes and handed them down until they were worn out. Children's clothes were made out of anything that still had some wear in it. One friend had a dress made out of an old shirt of her father's. I wore a pair of my cousin Robin's old shorts. Woollens were unravelled and knitted up again. Stripes and Fair Isles were very much in fashion for children's jumpers, as they would use up all the odd colours. Considering the difficulties, life in Mainstone went on fairly smoothly.

Our daily routine in the School House was regulated by the strong personalities of the two single ladies. After supper, when everything had been cleared away, we played games or listened to the wireless, the BBC Home service and Light programmes. We listened to everything: ITMA, the Brain's Trust, Elsie and Doris Walters, or Vera Lynn singing 'We'll meet again', which made my mother cry. In spite of her blindness Aunt Julia was good at games such as 'Word Making and Word Taking' (a kind of scrabble), chess or draughts, and we had a good many games together. I gained approval by picking up the stitches in my aunt's knitting - a vast, pale blue affair that was supposed to become a vest. I also learnt to knit and we often sat together, knitting busily.

She had a wonderful memory. She would listen to the news and be able to repeat it, word for word, to Miss Chopping when she came in from school. This impressed me greatly. The news was enormously important. I had to sit without moving when it was on while Aunt absorbed every bulletin. She liked to listen to articles from the paper being read aloud by Miss Chopping, while I held a skein of wool for her to wind a new ball. I would sit there, my arms aching, only understanding a little of what she read, but I caught the seriousness of her tone and was afraid. Phrases caught my attention: news of bombing raids in London, when in March several hundred enemy planes were reported overhead; of heavy casualties – over 21,000 since September; of Rommel in Africa; of fighting in Greece; of the plight of the Jews in Europe; of heavy losses at sea – five British ships were reported sunk in one operation. Soon after that it was decided not to give the details of losses any longer, as it was bad for public morale. In April Yugoslavia surrendered; on 20th of that month 712 planes were reported over London, their bombs causing total devastation. The Allies were evacuating Greece. Every day the news that came across the air was bewilderingly grim. Always we had in the back of our minds our dear family so far away in the vulnerable south east of England and wondered if we would ever see them again.

After five months Winston Churchill broke his silence. He spoke of the vital importance of American aid. 'We shall not fail or falter. We shall not weaken or tire... Give us the tools and we will finish the job.'

His words stirred people to stoical endurance. Of course our own news from home was terribly important to us. My father and mother wrote to each other constantly and my father sent me precious sweets and books. When I was ill my mother would keep me home from school and we would stay up in our bedroom by the fire. They were cosy times. I would sit up in bed while my mother read aloud. I grew to love books such as: 'Pooh Bear', 'Milly Molly Mandy', 'The Caravan Children' and 'Mary Plain'. My mother wrote to my father with all our news, letters that were full of plans to return home. She begged him to keep our things stored safely and perhaps find a place where it would be safe for us to live. But he was now no longer living in our lovely house and had taken rooms on a friend's farm. Sometimes the sound of music on the wireless would remind me of him and I would cry myself to sleep.

When I was well, however, I went to school. I quite liked it. I shared a desk with a girl called Gladys. She was a small, rosy-cheeked girl who came from a farm further up the valley. On my other side was a boy called Billie Bevan who was kinder than the other boys. My favourite lesson was writing. I carefully inscribed lines of letters in a shiny exercise book with my new pen or copied poems off the board then learnt them by heart, some of which I remembered long afterwards. There were two rooms, one for infants and one for the older children, of which I was one. Our classroom was small and dark. A large stove warmed it in winter and on wet days the room would become very fuggy with the steam which rose from the piles of clothing drying round the fire.

Many of the children arrived exhausted from their long walk over the hills from the outlying farms. Quite small children would leave home on dark winter mornings before it was properly light to struggle through the sodden countryside and arrive at school wet and weary. Before they could start work they would huddle round the stove to get warm and were often revived by a hot cup of cocoa. Beside the stove was Miss Chopping's desk and beside it on the wall was a large blackboard. Our desks facing it were made to seat two children. They had sloping wooden tops and inkwells in which we dipped our pens. These were filled up each week by the ink monitor.

The big boys sat at the back. They were nearly fourteen and ready to leave school. They were resentful of sitting in a classroom when they could do a man's work helping at home, and were often absent when it was a busy time on the farms. They were frequently disruptive and I took a somewhat perverse delight in seeing them get the cane. This cane Miss Chopping kept on her desk and wielded it with a short, sharp whizzing sound when the need arose. It seemed an entirely fair arrangement to me for all the annoyance they had caused. At the end of the afternoon we would fold our hands in prayer and sing a final hymn. Then if any of the lads had misbehaved they would be called out for punishment before they went home. They always seemed to take this in a cheerful and forgiving spirit and none of them ever seemed to hold a grudge against Miss Chopping for what they seemed to feel was only fair.

We had monitors for everything: book monitors, door monitors, nature-table monitors, coal monitors and chalk monitors. My favourite task was to be the nature-table monitor. Then I had to fill up the potted meat jars holding the different wild flower specimens with water, or put the birds' eggs on cotton wool. The boys collected the eggs and would think nothing of taking all the eggs from one nest and wringing the necks of the baby birds if they found them. I believe these were usually the young of magpies and jackdaws which they believed to be harmful, but I hated them for this.

Some of the boys were a rough bunch whose favourite pastime was to fight; or chase the girls and try to get their hands up their knickers. Some of the girls quite enjoyed this rough and tumble but I hung back and they never accosted me. Once though, when I was helping to pick cabbage white butterfly eggs off my aunt's cabbages with a boy called Wallace, who helped in the garden, he made me sniff lime up my nose and I was rushed indoors to wash it out before it could burn me horribly. On the whole though, the children were quite well behaved and good-natured. They made raffia mats for Christmas presents and practised carols in their sharp Shropshire voices. Miss Chopping, thumping on the piano with half its notes stuck or missing could not see what was happening behind her and practices often ended abruptly when she slammed down the lid of the piano and we were given lines to copy off the board instead.

It was after the terrible bombing of Liverpool, when for seven nights the city was under constant attack and thousands were made homeless, that the school received even more evacuees. Large numbers of children were sent to the country and emergency plans were made to receive them. They came from the most appalling conditions. They were frightened, filthy and quite unused to country ways. Many were verminous, covered with skin diseases and had to be fumigated before being sent to their new homes. Some of them had never bathed and were nervous of removing their clothes, which were often in rags and had to be burnt. It was hard enough to attend to their physical needs. Little time was given to their mental plight.

Everything was strange to them. The green countryside seemed empty and alien too. They found the silence at night and lack of streetlights and usual city sounds unnerving. They were used to shops just around the corner where they were sent to buy chips and cigarettes; neighbours nearby, and a local pub where they played about outside while their parents had a drink. They were terrified of dark trips to an outside lavatory at the bottom of the garden. Bed-wetting was frequent. They were unused to sitting down at the table for their meals and were quite unused to country food. They liked fish and chips, bread and margarine, beer and cheese, and lard on their bread. It was strange to find people who stayed at home with no nearby pub or cinema to go to and whose lives were ruled by the needs of their animals. Quite unused to animals and their ways, they had often never seen a chicken or a cow. Homesick for the familiar streets, many decided to return home. Some, however, stayed and when their first fright was overcome, grew to love their new surroundings and years later were still in touch with their wartime families.

When more evacuees arrived in Mainstone they were herded into the school to be sorted out. They sat there dazed and bewildered and waited. My mother and the other women who had gone along to help surveyed them with misgiving, but they could only feel desperately sorry for these children who had in many cases lost everything they possessed and often their homes and parents as well. Gradually they were cleaned up, new clothes were found and they were paired off with someone willing to take them.

With the school filling up with these new arrivals, my mother decided to keep me at home and teach me herself. She was nervous of my coming into contact with so much infection. Reports of behaviour among the boys, of which she did not approve, and the frequent disruption of lessons made her decide that I was better off at home where I would not fall behind or learn 'rough' ways. But this decision was frowned on by Aunt and Miss Chopping and it was not until some time later that it actually took place.

My mother longed to go back to Kent. She became more and more restless and unhappy. She wrote to my father nearly every day begging him to find some quiet place where we could return and set up home together again. Time after time she made suggestions and asked him about different areas and whether they would be safe. She seemed to think that a little place tucked away on Ashdown Forest, perhaps rooms on a farm there, might be away from the bombing. She asked him to find out if any such place was near an airport which might be a target, how much it would cost and whether there would be room to store our belongings. She wanted to know if it would be near enough for him to travel to work. Again and again she tried to make plans to travel back but one thing after another stopped her from returning. Eventually we did get as far as Shipston-on-Stour in the Midlands to stay with friends, but this did not turn out too well either and we were soon to return to Shropshire.

All this must have affected me and, although outwardly a happy child, I began to show signs of insecurity. For many years I suffered acute anxiety if any move was imminent. Even holidays caused me to retire to bed with a temperature. Bad news would make me run from the room to the safety of my bedroom. I longed for a settled home, safe and secure with a family round me. I longed to stay at a school long enough to make permanent friends. I longed for my father, his gentle teasing, endless games and the music which was so much a part of his life. I was tired of sharing other people's houses, toys and relations. I wanted to go home.

My Pembury friends in the hop fields. On the left is Alec McCowan (who was to become a celebrated actor of stage and screen), Bernar Waters, Jean (Alec's sister) and Susan Waters.

Chapter Seven

SHIPSTON ON STOUR

Spring 1941

It was in the spring of 1941 that my mother decided we needed a change from living at the School House. She had become very depressed and longed for a change of company and a little more comfort. She wrote constantly to my father trying to make plans to get home.

Eventually we went to Shipston-on-Stour where we had an invitation to stay with some friends. Arthur and Maisie had been close neighbours in Pembury who, with Duncan and Mary McCowan, and their children Alec and Jean, and George Prentice, a young curate who lived in digs nearby, we were to form lasting friendships which were to continue all our lives. Maisie and Arthur and their young daughter Heather were now living in Shipston. They sent us a warm invitation to come to stay with them, and feeling that it was a step nearer home, my mother gratefully accepted. We joined them in the April of 1941 and my parents made plans to meet there at Easter.

Maisie was a warm-hearted, motherly person who made us very welcome. They lived in a flat on the top floor of the rectory. After The School House everything seemed so warm and comfortable. The beds were soft, the linen beautifully clean, there was electricity and above all, as far as my mother was concerned, an easy chair to sit in. It was wonderful. I remember how kind they were and how Heather tried very hard to let me share her things. My mother enjoyed being nearer to civilisation. She went shopping and had her hair done. She talked about clothes with Maisie and reminisced about their life in Pembury. She wrote to my father planning his visit and explaining about the petrol that Arthur was able to get for him to make the journey.

When Maisie needed their room back for Heather to come home for the holidays, my mother decided to stay in the area for a while and we moved to a guesthouse owned by a Mrs Shaw about five miles from Shipston. This was only a temporary arrangement. My mother was undecided about what to do next. My father's brief visit was spoilt by anxious planning over the future.

Unfortunately we had found ourselves in a much more dangerous place than the quiet valleys of Shropshire. Night after night enemy planes roared overhead on their mission of destruction. Coventry was not far to the north of us and the noise of gunfire and bombs kept us awake. One night in April following the other terrible bombing in November, 200 planes dropped 330 tons of bombs and over 50,000 houses were damaged. The centre of Coventry and its beautiful cathedral of St Michael's were in ruins. The news of the war was very grim. Shipping losses were up 50% since March, so bad that Churchill told the information ministry to stop publishing details of the numbers of ships that were sunk. On the night of 16th April, London had one of the heaviest raids of the war. The devastation was tremendous. The news from the Mediterranean was also terrible, the evacuation of Greece described as a second Dunkirk. On 20th April there was another raid on London which involved over 700 planes, and the resulting fires were compared to the great fires of December 1940.

We heard that the London streets were impassable and that all the main line stations were closed. The light of a beautiful full moon only contributed to the nights of terror and destruction. News of heavy bombing came from Plymouth, Hull and Liverpool, where seven nights of continuous bombing led to the city being virtually cut off, as all the phone lines were down. Heavy raids from 237 bombers occurred in Birmingham, clearly heard by us in Shipston. Government leaflets appeared in the Home Counties telling people to leave while they could.

Again my mother was torn. My grandmother wrote begging her not to return but to stay away a little longer. She wrote to my father again trying to make plans, speaking of her faith that all would one day be well. Her hopes seemed to lie in the hope of a 'big offensive in the East' – the opening of the Russian front which people were expecting – which might ease the situation in the British Isles by occupying enemy forces elsewhere. But in the meanwhile...

By May we were once more back in Mainstone, this time at Reilth Farm and staying with the Deakins family. Our hopes of returning home and our longing to be reunited with my father were overshadowed by my mother's overpowering need for my safety. It was the grimmest time of the war. The blitz reached new peaks of horror and there were many casualties. The battle in the Mediterranean round Crete led to heavy losses. On 27th May came the shock of hearing that the Bismark was sunk. The following day the Allies began to evacuate Crete. On 22nd June Hitler attacked Russia. It was to be a long hard slog. People began to realize the war would not be over quickly, although most believed in ultimate victory. In October Leningrad surrendered, Kiev was captured and the Germans got nearer to Moscow. Little did we know that dear, music-loving Jens, my father's German friend of those dim days in Pembury, was fighting on the Russian front and was to become a prisoner of war. The Russians demanded a second front but this was not to happen until 1943. Long before then we would have returned to Kent, after another long spell in Shropshire.

Chapter Eight

REILTH FARM
May 1941

We knew the minute we arrived at Reilth Farm that we had come to a happy place. It was a Sunday afternoon and the Deakins family were gathered in the main living room where a long table was loaded with a substantial tea. The room was bright with firelight which shone on the highly-polished oak floor and wall panelling and reflected cheerfully in pieces of brass and copper round the huge fireplace. Large home-cured hams hung on hooks from the low beams above us. A huge silver teapot stood at one end of the table which was laid for at least a dozen people. I was accustomed to the frugal meals of the ration conscious occupants of the School House and I gazed in amazement at the laden table.

Huge piles of home-made bread and the pale unsalted butter which tasted quite different from the shop variety, round cheeses, slices of the home-cured bacon, fruit cakes and congress tarts oozing with jam, fruit flans overflowing with fruit and jelly and accompanied by large bowls of cream fetched from the dairy. It was a wonderful sight. The usual Sunday gathering of the whole family was in full swing. The room seemed full of laughter and the noise of their singsong Shropshire voices as they made us welcome. Sleeping cats were pushed aside and space was made for us on the deep old settle on one side of the fire where the black kettle, hanging on a chain, was just coming to the boil and spurting water with a hiss onto the flames below.

On the other side of the fire sat Mr Deakins. Dressed in his Sunday clothes, it was the only day in the week that he wasn't working from dawn to dusk. His was a large, well-run farm where the whole family was expected to pull its weight, but today he could sit and enjoy his rest. Mrs Deakins was watching the two eldest girls put the finishing touches to the table. She had prematurely white hair pulled into a neat bun, a handsome face and the shining dark eyes of the Welsh. Nancy and Mary rushed in and out of the room bringing even more food to the already-laden table. These two eldest girls, now nearly grown up, still lived at home and, we learnt later, did a great deal of work on the farm. Both were strong and full of laughter and high spirits, especially Mary, who at almost nineteen seemed to do the work of several strong men. Nancy, pretty and dark-eyed like her mother, was musical and played the piano and the organ in church each Sunday.

The water boiled and the silver teapot was filled and placed on the table and we all sat down. I was put next to Mrs Deakins who poured out the tea, gave orders to the girls as they flew about making sure everyone's cups and plates were constantly filled, coaxed me to eat and kept up a non-stop stream of conversation and bits of gossip in the high lilting tones of the Welsh borders.

Out in the fields at the Reilth with Martha where the horses were bringing in the harvest

Opposite me, on a long bench with their backs against the oak panelling, were four more of the family. The next two girls, Martha and Ada, were home for the weekend. During the week they attended Bishop's Castle High School and boarded with an Auntie who lived in the town. When they left school they both went off to do nursing and so I never knew them as well as other members of the family. Next came Gladys, nearer my own age, fair and sturdy with a big bow in her short hair. She went to Mainstone School while I was there and we became good friends. Beside her sat Margaret, the youngest of the family of seven, a tiny waif who promised to be very pretty when she grew up but who was at the moment rather delicate and often kept in when we were playing in the fields. She hardly spoke and ate very little, eyeing me with her big dark eyes from her side of the table. Edward, the only boy and a little older than me, sat near his father and ate all the tasty food his sisters piled on his plate.

The only boy among the seven surviving children, he was brought up knowing that, as the son, he would one day inherit the farm. He was at school in Mainstone too but spent a great deal of his time with his father in the fields, often doing the work of a man. He smiled at us shyly and sat quietly while his sisters chattered, concentrating on his plate.

I sat watching each member of the family in turn and, half listening to the buzz of conversation, I began to feel sleepy. I looked across at the row of friendly faces and round at the warm and welcoming room that was to become so familiar. All our meals were to be eaten here, with our backs against the panelling of the stairs that led to the upper floor. At supper time we would sit under the watchful eye of Mrs Deakins or one of the older girls and eat the bowls of bread and milk that were set out on the long shining table for us before we went to bed, then sliding off the bench we would murmur in turn, 'Please to excuse me and thank you for my nice meal', before leaving the table. Mrs Deakins believed in good manners and was a strict disciplinarian but she had a heart of gold and everyone loved her dearly.

The Reilth Farm was one of the largest farms in the Mainstone valley. The house was set on a rise above the lane that went on towards Cefn Einion and Clun. It was approached up a drive which, after passing through the gate off the road, rose sharply through a field, curving round the garden hedge to end in a cobbled area near the farm buildings. A tall pine tree stood at the top of the rise, at the place which was often the setting for the first sight of new arrivals or the parting, as someone left us. Straight ahead were the granary steps and

The Reilth Farmhouse

the big wooden gates which led into the farmyard proper. This yard was surrounded on all sides by the stone farm buildings in the middle of which was a high muck heap on which stray hens were usually scratching busily. To the right was the entrance to the stackyard which held several large stacks of straw, and where the buildings which housed many of the farm implements stood, alongside several carts and the trap in which Mrs Deakins went to market each Friday. Next to the sheds was a tall Dutch barn, an open building which held the huge quantities of hay and straw which were needed to see the animals through the long winters.

This yard was a fascinating place for children to play. We rolled in the soft straw at the bottom of the barn; slid down the stacks until we were shouted at for pulling down too much straw; climbed into the carts in search of eggs and kittens and to play hide-and-seek. It was a place of rustling secrets, of warm, sweetly-smelling dens where we could lie hidden in a golden womb of delight.

On the left as one stood under the pine tree was the house. Set in a garden, which consisted mainly of rhododendron bushes, it was a pleasant cream-washed building with an imposing porch on the front which was seldom used, as everyone went in and out through a narrow entrance which led through a small paved yard to the back door. Across the entrance the sheepdogs were often sprawled on the cobbles, waiting for Mr Deakins to come out and call them. In the middle of the yard was a hand pump which was in constant use. Beside it were slabs of slate on which buckets were stood, clothes rinsed, boots cleaned, vegetables prepared or chickens plucked. This helped to relieve the congestion at the kitchen sink in this busy household.

On one side of the yard, with a neat stack of kindling beside it, was the brick oven where once a week, a fresh supply of bread was baked. Straight ahead was the back door which led into the stone-flagged kitchen where a large black range needed constant tending. This was where most of the meals were prepared and the men ate during the week when, kicking off their boots by the door and washing their hands at the sink, they would sit down in their work clothes which still smelt strongly of the farm.

The solitary pine tree, setting for many arrivals and departures, is still there today

On Saturday nights a large galvanized bath was placed in front of the fire in which we all took turns to have our weekly dip. On other days the bath was used for

Mary in the yard with one of the horses having a well-earned Sunday rest

washing clothes or bread making and when not in use hung on a hook in the yard. Off the kitchen was the dairy which was always clean and cool. Here on narrow benches along the walls, pans of milk were left standing waiting for the cream to rise, and eggs were stored in racks waiting for market. Here also was the butter churn, a large wooden barrel set on a stand which was filled with cream and turned by a handle over and over until the butter set. In a little lobby outside the dairy door some steep back-stairs led to the first floor. Here also were two steps which led to the main living room in which we had first had tea. It was a house of sudden steps, of hidden corners and mysterious doors, wonderful for children's games but awkward for an adult to manage.

On each side of the living room were two smaller rooms which were only used on special occasions. One was a pleasant sunny parlour which had a door leading into the garden. It had much more delicate furniture, small tables on which stood silver-framed photographs, pretty chairs and a piano round which we gathered for the occasional sing-song. On the other side of the living room, up two more steps, was another parlour. This was a much more formal room and was seldom used. Later on my mother gave me my lessons here, and we sat at the polished table struggling with English grammar exercises and 'Stories from Foreign Lands' with which my mother tried to extend my somewhat limited education.

Upstairs the bedrooms led off a corridor. I don't remember much about them as I was seldom ill in this house and was far too busy out of doors to spend much time in my room. I remember large white coverlets, polished floors which creaked horribly and a washstand with its jug and basin in which we washed and cleaned our teeth. At the side of the house was a lean-to lavatory with a wooden seat which perched us above unmentionable depths into which it was best not to peer, and which were cleared out from the back of the building from time to time. Chamber pots were used in the bedrooms at night and emptied each morning.

Outside there was always something interesting going on. It was a busy farm - mostly sheep rearing - and the whole family worked very hard to maintain it. Sometimes Mr Deakins and Edward would ride off on their ponies to the high pastures to tend the sheep. They would be gone for several days and, meanwhile, the other farm animals needed feeding and looking after. Cows needed to be milked, pig swill to be boiled and fed to the pigs over the wall of their sty, chickens fed and things prepared for the weekly market. The work seemed endless.

Mary taught me to ride on Dolly in the field below the house

At certain times it was busier still: when sheep dipping or shearing was going on; at the season of hay time or harvest; when the turkeys and other poultry needed plucking for Christmas; or the fruit all ripened at once for jam making and bottling. Then everyone was at full stretch until the work was done. People would help one another at such times and the girls in the kitchen would be busier than ever feeding all the extra mouths. It paid to be on good terms with one's neighbours when everyone was so dependent on one another for help and so much of the work was done by hand.

On Sundays it was different. Only the essential work was done. Best clothes were worn and nearly the whole family would walk to the church, two miles away down the valley where Nancy played the organ. In the afternoon the family gathered for the large tea, a walk round the farm, a good exchange of local gossip and some entertainment, games or music. It was a happy noisy household and I loved it. From being an only child I became one of a large family. There was always laughter and fun and someone to play with, in spite of the hard work.

Mary took me under her wing. She was exactly ten years older than I was and we celebrated our next birthday together. At nineteen she was an invaluable help to the household and worked from morning to night without seeming to tire. She did a lot of the work indoors, relieving her mother of many of the heavy tasks: washing, ironing, butter-making, cleaning, cooking, and always with her loud laugh and cheerful ways. Outside too her work was hard: helping to milk the cows, feed the pigs and poultry, dip the sheep and get in the harvest. Everyone worked hard but it was Mary who seemed to throw herself into everything with so much enthusiasm.

I began to put on weight and look stronger. I spent as

much time as I could out of doors, playing endless games and watching things happen on the farm. My mother too seemed happier, and helped as much as she could. The lively company and easy-going ways kept her from feeling so lonely. She wrote to my father telling him how she loved to see everything that was going on. The family were all very kind to us and tried in many ways to make us feel at home. That summer we did our lessons at a table in the garden. On one occasion, while we were sitting there and I was trying to learn a poem by heart with most of my attention on the sounds of the other children returning from school, Edward overcame his shyness and brought me some wild strawberries which he had picked on the way home.

I think my mother must have decided to let me return to school in the summer, for I remember walking there with Gladys along the lane and across the bridge spanning the stream. The lanes were full of wild roses and honeysuckle, and no cars came along to disturb us. As we went we picked wild flowers for the nature table and hunted for birds nests in the tall uncut hedges.

One day we took a short-cut through a field and nearly came to grief. The bulls in the neighbourhood were often let out and roamed about harmlessly most of the time. On this occasion there was a bull in the field which was hidden from us by some trees until we were in the centre of the field. Suddenly he saw us. He was in a bad temper. His tail stretched out stiffly and he began to paw the ground, a sure sign, we thought, that he was about to charge. The nearest gate seemed miles away and we ran for the shelter of some tall bracken, hoping that if he could no longer see us he might forget us. Luckily this is what happened, and we crawled safely to the gate. We were rightly afraid of him, however, and did not go that way again.

It was in the July of that year that my father, who had managed to save enough petrol for the journey, joined us for a short holiday. He looked white and strained when he first arrived after the long drive from Kent. It was a cross-country journey in those days and there had been no signposts to help him find the way. All these had been removed in case of invasion. Our small old Morris car was loaded with all the things we had asked him to bring as, by this time, my mother had decided to remain in Shropshire until the autumn, when she felt the fear of invasion would have passed. My parents had made a pact to try not to spoil the short time together by making endless plans and worrying about the future. The weather was good and it was wonderful to be able to show my father all our favourite places.

Gradually, in the peace of the valley, the strained look left his face and he began to enjoy himself. He had brought his paints and sketchpad and sat happily in the garden making a sketch of the house. Nights of unbroken sleep free from the sound of sirens and the long hours of fire-watching helped him to relax. The family loved him. Mrs Deakins fed him huge meals and packed up loads of things for him to take on his return. To cheer him up the girls teased him unmercifully, and got him to join in their games.

In the evenings we gathered round the piano while he played and we sang. On the Sunday he took over from Nancy at the church organ and as my mother's lovely voice sang the familiar hymns I wished it could go on forever. But the week came to an end only too quickly and it was time to wave him goodbye. We stood under the pine tree and watched his little car disappear as he set off to face the following months alone in war-torn Kent. While the news of the war grew steadily worse our hopes of joining him seemed even more remote. I know my mother found it very hard to carry on after he had gone and we both had a difficult time trying to be brave. Soon however we settled back into the routine which we had made for our lives here and his brief visit seemed like a dream.

Chapter Nine

OUR DAILY BREAD

1941–42

Butter-making was usually Mary's job. Once a week she would disappear into the cool interior of the dairy, give the cream a final stir, and pour it into the scalded churn. Then would come the rattling sound of the churn revolving and the soft swishing sound of the cream within it. On some days it turned quickly and there would be a sigh of relief as Mary came to the door to tell her mother. Sometimes she would be gone for a long time before the slopping sound was replaced by soft thuds as the cream separated and the solid lumps of butter began to form in the whey. The whey was then drained off to be given to the pigs and cold water was added. The globules of butter formed into a solid mass which was rinsed several times before being turned out onto a slate slab to be beaten with the wooden butter-pats until all the liquid had been extracted. Then it was formed into slabs, weighed, and set on one side on the cool shelves to wait for market day. There was a kind of tension in the house until the butter turned. It was as though everyone was listening for the sound to change before we could all relax. Some said it was the weather that caused it to go well or badly. Perhaps it was the condition of the cream. Maybe Mary herself did something different. I know I was glad when my friend could be herself again and perhaps have time to play.

Bread too was made once a week in the brick oven in the backyard. It was mixed in the galvanized bath in which, on Saturdays, we had our baths. I loved the smell of the yeast as it stood frothing on the stove before being added to the flour, and I watched, fascinated, as the whole lot was turned out and pounded vigorously before being left to rise on the side of the range. Usually the yeast did its work and the dough would grow and puff itself up until it had doubled in size, but just as it seemed about to overflow onto the stove, Mrs Deakins would turn it out onto a board to knead it again. It always seemed a pity to knock it down, but then it was divided into pieces and left to rise a second time. Meanwhile one of the girls had been heating the oven with plenty of dry kindling until the bricks glowed red and then white and it was ready, at just the right moment, to receive the risen dough. The loaves were pushed into the hot interior on a long handled implement shaped like a shovel. This had to be done swiftly before the heat was lost or the dough lost its buoyancy.

When they were cooked, the loaves, risen into great mounds of golden perfection, were removed onto a rack to cool. Coming home from school to find the air filled with the sweet smell of baking, we needed no one to hurry us in to tea. Thin oval slices, spread with pale butter and home-made blackberry jelly had a taste beyond description.

In those days many farmer's wives supplemented their house-keeping with any money they could make out of the poultry. Egg production and the rearing of birds for the table was a welcome source of income which could be made while managing a busy house and family. While we were at the Reilth, Mrs Deakins had chickens, ducks, geese, guinea fowl and turkeys.

The turkeys seemed to cause her a lot of trouble. She would often despair at their awkward ways. 'If there's anything they can do to kill themselves they'll do it,' she cried, as her precious birds insisted on committing suicide with unfortunate regularity. When they did grow, they became her pride and joy and the source of much admiring comment. 'Huge birds they are,' she would exclaim, 'and with that much meat on them!' They were cosseted and petted until the final day came when they were considered to be ready. Mr Deakins, taking over the task of executioner, would disappear into a shed where, one by one, they were dispatched and hung by the feet in a lordly row, their heads hanging despondently floorwards.

Then came the time for plucking and trussing the big, beautiful birds. Mrs Deakins and the girls would sit for hours plucking, surrounded by a sea of feathers. They would emerge every now and then, with white down in their hair and clinging to their eyebrows, to drink a hurried cup of tea. There would be an urgency about it all until it was done and the turkeys were laid out with bulging bosoms, trussed and ready in time for the Christmas market. I didn't care about the turkeys. I had been rather afraid of them as they stalked about gobbling loudly and shaking their feathers. They could be quite fierce.

I did feel rather sorry for the geese who appeared to be such a devoted family. They were a familiar sight grazing in the field or preening themselves by the stream. I watched sadly as the young ones were taken away and only the gander and one or two of his wives were left, wandering about and calling disconsolately. The geese were more difficult to kill and to pluck. I hated the sounds of flapping and squawking as their necks were broken over a pole and I kept well out of the way while this was being done. It needed a strong arm to do it swiftly and humanely. Suggestions were made as to the best way to pluck them. 'Iron them,' one elderly aunt suggested, 'that loosens the feathers.' 'Dip them in boiling water,' someone else suggested; but Mrs Deakins, capable hands planted firmly on the soft grey bodies, soon dealt with them, and they joined the turkeys in the cool dairy to wait for market day.

Chickens and ducks were culled at any time of year, one lot succeeding another as they reached maturity. Feathers flew everywhere as we tried to help. The best were stuffed into an old pillowcase to be used later for refurbishing the pillows and eiderdowns on the beds. Most of the hens were Rhode Island Reds or White Leghorns. They had the free run of the farm and were to be seen pecking and scratching happily in the stackyard and around the buildings. There was always some scattered grain, or juicy worms on the muckheap. Heaven help anyone who left the granary door open and let them into the grain stored there.

It was often my job to collect the eggs. It was a treasure hunt. I got to know where the nests were likely to be. Armed with a basket and dressed in a Fair Isle jersey, shorts and my Wellington boots, I would crawl into far corners of the build-ings or into a cart or piece of machinery to find a secret nest. Sometimes I came across a nest that had had eggs added to it for several days without being discovered, and I would collect a dozen eggs at once. Sometimes these had been left too long and we had to find out if they were still edible by putting them in water to see if they floated, which meant they were bad; or sank, at which they were pronounced fit to eat. Occasionally a nest would remain undiscovered and a broody hen would manage to hatch her chicks undisturbed. Then she would appear, proudly leading her small family out to join the other hens and they would scratch around copying their mother. The best eggs were put in trays to wait for market day. The seconds were used for cooking, their golden yolks giving the cakes and puddings a rich colour and a wonderfully smooth texture.

At Easter we children were given one egg each which we boiled with gorse flowers to turn their shells yellow, and ate them for our breakfast on Easter morning. Chocolate Easter eggs were few and far between in wartime and took some of our precious sweet coupons.

Every day at about the same time Mrs Deakins would fill a bucket with corn and go out to feed the hens, throwing it to them with a broad sweep of her arm and calling to them, 'Chuck, chuck, choo'. This would be an opportunity for her to look them over to see if any were sick or had stopped laying. She said that those in lay had bright red combs. As it grew dark the hens would put themselves to bed in the hen house where, with a lot of shuffling and the odd squawk, they would settle down for the night. Then the cry, 'Has anyone shut up the fowls?' would often cause an anxious rush in the dark to do so before the fox came round. Tales of foxes getting in and killing all the hens at once, leaving them scattered around uneaten, were quoted, and the task of shutting them up safely had to be done every night whatever the weather.

In the spring one of the big Rhode Island Reds went broody. She sat, her feathers fluffed out, sinking into a torpid state, refusing to leave the nest. 'They make very good mothers,' I was told. I watched as she was put into a coop on her own. When she had settled down, a dozen brown eggs were gently put under her and we were told to leave her in peace. I waited excitedly for the three weeks to pass until the eggs were due to hatch. The hen guarded the clutch fiercely and pecked out at anyone who disturbed her. One day when I had almost given up hope, Mary reached carefully under her soft feathers and, avoiding the sharp beak, drew out a warm egg and held it to my ear. There was a faint cheeping sound coming from inside the shell. She put it back gently. A few days later there was the sound of chipping and a small hole appeared. We waited, not daring to interfere as the chick enlarged the hole with the special tip it had developed on its beak. Every now and then it seemed to give up the struggle and we were tempted to help. Eventually the hole was large enough for a few damp feathers to be seen and then the shell cracked in two and a damp, crumpled ball of feathers appeared. It was nothing like I expected, but soon, as the little creature dried off and uncurled, it turned into the yellow ball of fluff that I had seen on the Easter cards. Gradually all the eggs hatched and little heads appeared from beneath the hen's warm feathers and beady eyes surveying the world in a knowing fashion.

When they had all hatched and grown confident enough to run around, the hen was free to get up and stretch herself, after her long confinement. Then clucking in a motherly fashion she scratched about while the chicks ran around like small mechanical toys, chirping loudly, as they followed her.

After a few days the chicks were sexed. The cockerels were then kept separately to be fattened up for table, the pullets used to replenish the stock or sold as chicks, or later as point-of-lay pullets. They soon grew out of their fluffy babyhood. They became leggy and started to grow their adult plumage.

There were ducks too on the farm. Their eggs had deep yellow yolks which were good for cooking. The flavour was considered by some to be rather strong. They were also often suspected of causing food poisoning, although it was said they were only dangerous if the water where the ducks swam was polluted. As these ducks spent their time on the fast-running brook, I expect they were quite safe.

The geese only laid for a short time each year. They made a terrific fuss about it. About the beginning of February they would all begin to make a large mound of straw in a corner of one of the buildings. This took some time and involved much cackling and squabbling. Several of the geese then took possession and, ousting the weaker members of the flock, would begin to lay their eggs. These they covered carefully every time they left the nest, with mud and straw. The gander grew very possessive at this time and stood guard, attacking anyone who approached the nest ferociously with a great deal of hissing and wing flapping. The goose eggs were large, pure white and had very tough shells. The geese never seemed to notice when some eggs were missing. One or two were removed by Mary each day until it was decided to let them settle down and hatch the remainder. They were haphazard mothers and often let their eggs go cold. When the goslings did hatch they were great favourites of ours. They were lovely little things covered with a short, soft, greenish down. It was a special treat to be allowed to hold one carefully and feel its strange webbed feet clinging to our fingers.

Another source of meat was rabbit. There were usually one or two of these strung by their hind feet and dripping blood from their poor noses, hanging by the back door. When no one was looking I would stroke their soft fur and run my fingers along their cold ears. Once or twice I was given one of their tails to keep. It was sad, but after they had been skinned and cleaned and cooked with carrots and potatoes the smell of rabbit stew soon made me forget my scruples and enjoy a delicious meal.

Pigeon pie was a favourite too. It had the advantage of culling the pigeons, which flew down in large numbers to steal any newly planted crops. The birds were only small. The meat was often cut off before they were cooked and only the breast and legs used. Topped with pastry and plenty of gravy and with some redcurrant jelly, it was very good.

A few pigs were kept in a sty at the back of the house. These were fed on a mixture of skimmed milk, small potatoes, household scraps and meal. They were friendly creatures but we were warned they could give a bad bite. When they were fed they would push roughly against anyone who entered their sty and, if they were unprepared, would knock them off their feet in the rush to get to the trough. A sow can have as many as ten or twelve piglets at one time. A farrowing bar is put in the sty to prevent her rolling on them as she turns.

One night we were told we could go out to watch some piglets being born. We stood very quietly on the fence. By the light of a lantern we watched as the tiny creatures appeared, counting to ourselves, 'one, two, three.... ten, eleven, twelve!' It was an amazing sight as the sow lay supine, grunting softly as each small pink baby emerged. After only a few minutes each piglet would wriggle round to where her teats were waiting in a welcoming row. Soon they had all attached themselves to this bountiful supply of milk and were sucking contentedly like a line of small pink bolsters, their curly tails wriggling happily. They seemed to enjoy being picked up and with their firm little bodies, funny faces and curly tails, were nice to cuddle. But they quickly grew big and rough and we were warned to keep out of their way.

Once or twice a year a pig was killed. When this happened it was quite an event. Pigs are intelligent animals. It must have known what was about to happen, as it took several people to push it, squealing, into the backyard to stand by the pump where everything was in readiness. The dogs had been shut up but were barking wildly, which must have added to the poor creature's confusion. We children had been told to keep out of the way. It was Mary who joined the group by the pump and who, after the pig had been killed, held the basin to catch the blood which gushed from the gash that had been made in its throat. Huge amounts of hot water had been made ready in the kitchen. The carcase was scalded. Nearly-boiling water was poured over it and it was scrubbed and scraped to remove all the outer skin and the bristles. It was then split down the middle, the innards removed, and divided into manageable pieces to be taken inside to be dealt with. Some of course was used as pork but some needed to be salted down and stored. These pieces were rubbed hard with salt and then left buried in salt and rubbed again every three or four days. After two or three weeks they were ready to be hung from the beams in the living room where they were stored for at least six months before they were ready to eat. The bacon was fat and salty but extremely tasty. Nothing was wasted. All the parts of the pig's carcase had its uses and was an important source of food for the family.

The shortage of sugar was always a problem. It was possible to get extra to make jam. This was one thing my mother could help with. The Reilth was a centre for jam making in the district and twice a week in that season women would gather there to lend a hand. Any kind of fruit was used. Excursions were made along the hedges to gather blackberries to make into jelly. Blackcurrants and gooseberries were picked from bushes in the gardens. Strawberries and raspberries were highly prized, but there was not such an abundance of these fruit as we had known in Kent. Rhubarb or marrow preserve was made more tasty by the addition of ginger. Elderflowers and whinberries too were gathered on our trips out into the countryside.

Gladys and I were often roped in to help pick the fruit. We worked with backs bent double, our legs stung by nettles, to gather every last one. Then we would sit at the table in the kitchen, listening to the lilting voices of the helpers as they exchanged gossip over a cup of tea, and nipping off the stalks of the gooseberries with a pair of nail scissors or hulling the glistening piles of strawberries, odd ones of which, every now and then, were slipped surreptitiously into our mouths. Large preserving pans stood on the stove and scented steam rose in clouds. The precious sugar was added and the whole lot brought to the boil. After a while some of the mixture was put on a saucer and left to cool until, as a finger was drawn across, it wrinkled and was declared ready to set. Then the warmed

On horseback with Dolly and Mary

jars were filled and Gladys and I wrote labels for them in our best writing. 'Raspberry 1941.'

The satisfaction of seeing the rows of gleaming, neatly labelled jars made up for all the hard work. Fruit like pears, plums or tomatoes, were preserved in kilner jars and stored for the winter. Before the days of freezing this was the only way to keep them. Eggs were kept in isinglass in deep earthenware crocks. Runner beans were salted down; green tomatoes, apples and beans were made into pickles and chutney. Onions were pickled in vinegar. There were many ways to help the food shortage, especially in the country.

Of course sugar, tea, sweets, petrol and clothes were still rationed, but as the farm work was mainly done with horses, and a pony and trap was still quite often used, cars were seldom seen in the valley and petrol rationing did not worry us unduly. As for clothes, we had very few occasions when smart clothes were needed and were quite content to wear anything to keep us warm. Altogether we were very lucky. Our 'daily bread' was given to us generously. It was very hard work for those involved. My mother and I will never cease to be grateful to those kind people who shared it with us.

Chapter Ten

DANCING IN HOBNAILS
1941–42

One of the things I remember most about living at the Reilth was the noise and laughter of that vigorous and fun-loving family. As an only child whose health had often given my mother a good excuse to keep me at home, I had very little experience of family life or the rough and tumble of mixing with other children. I loved it. 'Running wild', an expression my mother used to describe the freedom of my life there, was an intoxicating experience.

As the weeks passed I grew strong and healthy. My illnesses of the previous winter were almost forgotten. There was any number of ways in which we amused ourselves, many of which were closely connected with farm life. The country-side round about was a never-ending source of enjoyment and we roamed safely in the fields and woods, never far from home but with a sense of freedom which is largely missing for children today.

On the way home from school we stopped by the bridge that crossed over the stream where the rushing water disappeared dizzily into the cool depths below us. With shoes kicked off and our dresses hitched up we paddled yelling with delight as the freezing water crept over our legs. The stream was fast-flowing and shallow. Its water glistened as it slid over the brown pebbles or ran, dark and mysterious, under the overhanging trees. Fish lurked in the shadowy pools and dragonflies hovered, their wings bright in the sunlight. In places it was almost hidden by thick undergrowth, in others grassy banks sloped down to where the cattle drank. Its little pebbly beaches were places of endless enchantment. The stones were warm in the sun and flat enough to be comfortable under our bare toes.

Every moment of those long summer days was spent out of doors. We younger children played endless imaginative games in the garden, using the rhododendron bushes as 'houses' so often, that we were turned out because the roots were becoming damaged by our pounding feet. Then we ran helter-skelter up the little hill behind the house and slid headlong downwards over the dry grass on tin trays. This was almost as fast as when we slid down on sledges in the winter, but we were much more likely to hurt ourselves as there was no bed of snow to soften our fall, and many grazed knees were the result.

At the top of the bank was a large old tree under which the ground had been worn smooth by sheltering sheep. This was a favourite place of ours. From here it was possible to see over the farm buildings below, from which came the comforting sound of voices, and across the fields, to the far side of the valley. Here we would sit and talk, play games or make up stories, twisting the rough odds and ends of sheep's wool between our fingers and making 'cat's cradles', until the lengthening shadows, the sound of Mrs Deakins feeding the hens, or the mournful cry with which the cows were summoned in for milking echoed round the valley, and we knew it was time for us to go in for tea.

The summer just before I was nine, Mary taught me to ride. In my Fair Isle jersey and a pair of my cousin Robin's shorts, which was my usual attire, I proudly mounted old Dolly, a bay pony of about thirteen hands. She was a sturdy mountain pony often used by Mr Deakins to ride up to the high pastures to look at the sheep, or by Mary for bringing in the cows. She was fifteen years old, docile and friendly, and well-used to children on her broad back. Unfortunately on the first occasion, Mary, who was leading me round the field below the house, let go of the bridle to get a twig from the hedge and Dolly, catching sight of it out of the corner of her eye, decided she had had enough and broke into a trot and then into a canter.

The stream was fast-flowing and shallow, its water glistened as it slid over the brown pebbles

The girth which at first had fitted so snugly round her fat stomach had, as she exercised, worked loose. Consequently as Dolly's pace quickened, the saddle began to slip and soon, with me still clinging on desperately, I was hanging underneath the pony, frightening Dolly to such an extent that she bolted for the safety of her stable. I remember the sight of her flying hooves very near my head before I fell off. We were all rather shaken but, in true horsemanship tradition, I was put straight back on.

Soon I learnt to ride quite well, something I was to enjoy throughout my childhood. Many long sunny days of that summer of 1941, while the war raged on, were spent in the fields, helping to toss the hay and piling it into mounds or standing the prickly sheaves of corn into stooks ready for the wagon. Soon tiring of the hot work, we would run among the haycocks, or go to paddle in the stream while the adults worked on as the shadows lengthened over the fields and the wagons seemed to

Often on a Friday Mrs Deakins would set off in the pony and trap loaded with provisions for sale in the weekly market at Bishop's Castle

fill more slowly, pulled by the sweating horses. About teatime someone would appear with jugs of tea which was drunk in the shade of hedges, where wild roses and honeysuckle gave way to red hips and haws as the year drew on.

The carts were drawn by horses. Heavy and cumbersome, it took two horses to pull them over the uneven ground. In the morning the work was done by Flower and Jolly, two quiet bays who saved their strength by working quietly and steadily. In the afternoon, however, two young greys took over who were apt to get excited and waste their energy with unnecessary fuss. Guiding these two through the narrow gateways was a difficult task and tempers were inclined to become frayed as precious time was lost. In the evening Flower and Jolly took over again and the work went on more calmly.

Load after load was brought back and stacked, and time after time we went back to the fields in the empty dray, squealing with laughter as we were flung to and fro as it lurched over the uneven ground. Our way led up a track, just wide enough for the horses, between the sweet smelling hedges and banks of purple willow herb, under great oak trees and hazels, whose nuts were just forming and whose soft branches brushed the wagon as we went by. The smell of the hot dry wood of the empty cart, the sweet smell of horses and of the leather harness and the unforgettable scent of newly-made hay all surrounded us. The sounds of the hooves on the rough land, the creak of harness, and rumble of the huge wooden, iron-clad wheels accompanied each journey. To the adults it may have been a time of unremitting hard work but to us it was paradise.

After the hay the corn was cut and the binder went round and round the fields until only a small patch of corn was left standing. Then all the men would stand with their guns ready while the dogs were sent in to flush out the rabbits who

In the stream at Mainstone with Margaret,
Gladys and some other friends

ran in all directions trying to reach the safety of the hedges.
Behind the slow-moving binder, the women and children
worked hard, dragging the heavy sheaves to stand them in
stooks to dry, leaning against each other. Then glistening as
they caught the rays of the setting sun, brittle stems rustling,
dried by the wind, they were heaved onto the carts on the end
of long pitchforks wielded deftly by the strong brown arms of
the men and by the older girls, whose supple figures in their
light, bright dresses belied their strength.

Eventually, after the corn had been threshed, some of the
straw was stacked in the big Dutch barn and so began an exhila-
rating game of climbing high up into the rafters and jumping into
the loose straw far below. As the stack grew higher, so more and
more daring was needed for the jump as we launched ourselves
into mid-air, to land safely on the barn floor.

The horses were a very important part of the farm
economy. Because of the hilly nature of the land, the fields
were small and inaccessible to large machinery. The petrol

shortage too meant that many supplies were brought in by horse and cart and it was a rare sight to see a car in the valley.

The horses were of great interest to my mother and me. It was wonderful to see them working with such patience and strength. Their great shiny bodies and heavy hooves, beautiful manes and large sad eyes fascinated us. It was a wonderful sight to watch them coming back over the fields with the laden carts, their harness gleaming, tossing their great heads at the marauding flies. In the depths of winter they were kept in and had very little exercise. Occasionally we watched from the granary door, high above the yard, while they were let out below us. Excited by their freedom after being shut in their stable, they broke out of their usual slow plod to gambol around, shaking their heads and kicking up their huge feet, which made a loud clatter on the cobbles as they chased each other round in a very undignified way.

In July it was my ninth and Mary's nineteenth birthday. We planned a joint celebration and as it approached I began to get excited, especially as my father was hoping to be there. My mother wrote to him asking him to bring a large basket of strawberries for the birthday tea. She knew that strawberry picking would be in full swing on the farms round our home in Kent and that it would be a special treat for the whole family in Mainstone. She also asked him about a present for me. The Deakins family were planning to give me a Bible and she said she thought perhaps a prayer book with coloured pictures, together with a small bag of boiled sweets, would do nicely; and for Mary a coloured belt or hair band. I cannot recall many details of my birthday, but I do remember the happiness of having my father there for his holiday and the close feeling I had with Mary because we shared this special day. Mary gave me a great deal of much-needed attention and often took me with her as she went round the farm. Always talking and laughing, she was fun to be with, and a wonderfully reassuring companion for a small girl who had lost much of her own security. Dark and slim, like her mother, and endlessly busy and active, she must have made an excellent farmer's wife when she later married another farmer and lived near Montgomery.

On winter evenings we often gathered in the small sitting room. Nancy would play the piano and we would sing. On one occasion we began dancing and Mr Deakins, in white shirt and black waistcoat, caught hold of me and whirled me round. Unfortunately he had forgotten that he was still wearing his hobnail boots and we slipped on the polished floor sending a small table flying and breaking a pretty vase. Nancy played quite well and would rattle off the well-known tunes at great speed. We sent off for the 'News Chronicle Song Book' and there was great excitement when it arrived. It had a brown cover with gold lettering and we opened it with pride. All the old favourites were there: 'The Meeting of the Waters' which reminded us of our valley, 'The Minstrel Boy', 'All Through the Night', 'David of the White Rock' and 'Shenandoah'. Then the hymns: 'The Lord is my Shepherd', 'Jesu lover of my soul', or 'Abide with me', which always brought tears to my mother's eyes as it was a great favourite of my grandmother's and we could still hear her strong, quavering voice rising above the sound of the organ in the Tabernacle in Lewes each Sunday. Then when my father came and played, he made the old piano sound glorious, although many of the notes stuck and it was rather out of tune.

Sometimes, for a little while, it was difficult to remember there was a war on. Farmhouse food was plentiful and the peace only broken by the drone of planes overhead. Then would come the time when my father had to leave us once more and letters or the occasional phone call were again our only means of keeping in touch. My mother's letters were still full of her anxieties about what to do for the best. They were somehow more innocent and naive than they would be today. Access to news, without the benefit of television, was limited. Trust in our leaders was absolute. A true realisation of the terrible things that were happening did not come until years later when details of the atrocities and the vast scale of the destruction were more widely known.

In spite of the worsening situation, hope for the end of the war and ultimate victory was always there. My mother's plans changed frequently, often thwarted by further fear of invasion or illness. As the summer days stretched into autumn, her plans to return home became more urgent. After five moves within a year, sharing other people's houses, she was determined to be reunited with my father before the winter and to find a more settled kind of existence.

The horses worked hard every day pulling the farm machinery

Chapter Eleven

MARKET DAY
1941–42

Market day was the climax of a week of preparation and hard work. As Friday drew near, the shelves in the dairy grew more and more crowded. Pats of butter, with moisture still oozing slightly from their pale yellow flesh, each slab finished off neatly with patterns made with the butter pats and sitting on a sheet of greaseproof paper, stood waiting. Eggs were piled in bowls, white shading to dark brown, plain or speckled. It was possible, Mary said, to tell which hen had laid each one; gathered from barn and straw-stack, they were highly prized for their size and the rich quality of their golden yolks. Day-old chicks, ducklings and goslings, trussed poultry, jars of preserve, bottled fruit, jam, chutney and pickles, bread, cakes and pies, cream and cheeses, and baskets of fruit – all were made ready in their season for the weekly market. The larger livestock was sent by lorry or driven over the night before, but all the smaller items went with Mrs Deakins in the trap or were taken on the once-weekly bus.

Our nearest town, Bishop's Castle, where the weekly cattle and produce market was held, was four and a half miles away. Here everyone in the district took their goods, and did their shopping. For people who spent their time on isolated farms, often out of sight of their nearest neighbour, this contact was something to look forward to. They bought the things needed for the coming week and caught up with all the news as they gathered in the market or stopped for a cup of tea. The busy little town of Bishop's Castle was originally called Lydbury Castle but changed its name when it was given to the Bishop of Hereford.

There is a story of King Ethelbert of East Anglia who fell in love with Alfreda, daughter of the Mercian king Offa who built the dyke. Her father was all in favour of the match but the Queen was jealous and plotted to kill her daughter's lover. She invited him to her room where he was told to sit on a certain seat. This had been especially prepared over a trap door. He fell into a pit below and was stabbed to death by the guards. The murdered king was buried in Hereford and canonized as a saint. His shrine was visited by pilgrims seeking a cure. Among those restored to health was Egwin Shakehead, the Saxon Lord of Lydbury, who was cured of palsy. In gratitude he gave his manor to the Bishop of Hereford and so Bishop's Castle was named. The castle was destroyed during the civil war but by this time the town had grown up round it and gained a charter. The Friday market was started in 1292. In 1861 Parliament approved a scheme for a railway line to Bishop's Castle which was to continue to Montgomery. Although construction began in 1863, it ran into difficulties with the local landowners and did not open until three years later.

The train must certainly have made it easier to reach this part of the world. The line ran to Craven Arms following the river Onny which it crossed six times. Trains were pulled by two engines named Perseverance and Progress. The track, however, had a history of difficulties. Once floods washed a bridge away. Sheep often blocked the line, and once a train uncoupled from the engine and started off by itself and was only stopped by the quick action of the guard. The company ran into financial difficulties and went bankrupt soon after its opening, but trains continued to run until 1935. If only it had continued, it would have made the visits of my father, and Edward Garrett and Kath's husband Jack, so much easier. The closest they could come when paying us a visit was Craven Arms, several miles distant. Jack solved this problem by bringing his bicycle with him and cycling from the station but it was a hard end to his long journey.

Our only public transport was the weekly bus which went from Mainstone to Bishop's Castle on market day. If we wanted to go into town shopping, my mother and I would catch it from outside the school. It was always crowded with farmers' wives, sitting with loaded baskets on their laps and the occasional crate of live chickens, rabbits or even a lamb cluttering up the aisle – their voices raised above the sound of the engine as they caught up on the week's news.

The bus's progress was a leisurely affair. Every few miles it would stop at the end of some track and anxious voices would call 'Is Mrs Price (or Jones or Evans) coming today?' 'She'll be late, what with her Susan being away.' 'She'll be coming for sure. She don't want to miss the fun.' 'We'll wait,' the bus driver would say resignedly. A small figure would appear struggling towards the bus under a load of bags and baskets, balancing a cake tin carefully in both hands. 'Here she comes.' 'She's never missed yet.' 'I expect that's Susan's cake for the W.I. stall. A good cook she is, like her mother.' 'And her mother before that.' The woman would struggle aboard to much cheering and off we would go again.

Getting up a hill was something of a problem and we often waited with bated breath to see if the old vehicle would get its load up the steep incline. We would go slower and slower with everyone tensing in their seats and willing the old bus forward. Reaching the top, a sigh of relief went round, and there was a cheer as we started off down the other side.

When the weather was reasonable, Mrs Deakins would prefer to go into town in the pony and trap. The pony that pulled this vehicle was called Tommie. He was thirty years old and his progress was slow and stately, but he could still manage a smart trot on the level stretches. Going downhill, a drag was put on the wheels to stop the trap pushing him too fast from behind. Going uphill we were often asked to dismount to ease his load and we would walk up the hill behind the trap, sometimes picking wild strawberries as we went. On many days, however, it was a cold form of transport and we would wrap up very well and take thick rugs to put over our knees. It had been known for Mrs Deakins to take a hot water bottle on which to warm her hands which grew very cold holding the reins. The trap held about four people, one in the front beside the driver and two facing backwards. Round our feet was stacked the precious cargo of goods for the market.

On reaching the town, everyone would go their separate ways. The men had gone in earlier and spent the day at the cattle market at the bottom of the town. They usually had their midday meal together in the upper rooms of a pub. Mrs Deakins would leave the pony and trap at Uncle Dick Robinson's yard and go off to deal with all her produce.

My mother and I would go in search of clothing, writing paper, needle and thread, or a much-dreaded visit to the dentist. The dentist's surgery was at the top of the steep main street which led from the Parish church at the bottom of the town up towards the Castle Hotel at the top. In the centre of the rather dark little room stood the chair which was operated by a foot pedal. The drill swung overhead on a long arm. No high speed painless drill then but a slow, noisy grinder which vibrated in one's mouth, quite literally setting one's teeth on edge. My mother seemed to suffer a great deal every time she went. On one occasion when she had had toothache for some time, she decided to have the tooth out. It was a difficult extraction which proved too much for the poor man. My mother was left with the tooth half in and half out while he went for help from a colleague who then proceeded to complete the operation in his place.

These visits did not deter us from spending our precious sweet coupons on a supply to last us over the coming week. There were not many sweets: I think I was allowed two a day but they were highly prized when crisps, ice creams, fizzy drinks or choc-bars were mainly unknown. The sweets were displayed in large glass jars and it was always a serious business deciding which to choose: barley sugar, acid drops, dolly mixtures which went a long way because they were so small, highly coloured boiled sweets or humbugs. My favourites were the golden, angular humbugs which came in tins. The loose sweets were put in little paper bags and after a short while in a pocket would melt slightly and stick together. My mother's favourite was Fry's peppermint cream chocolate or plain dark chocolate but this took up too many points for me. Our supply was often supplemented by parcels from my father who would forego his own ration to send it to us. Once we had a parcel of sweets from our cousins in Australia. It weighed very heavily and must have cost a lot to send. It was a huge hard block of very sweet stuff rather like a cross between coconut ice and concrete but I was tremendously excited when the parcel came. It also included some beautiful red and blue wool which my mother knitted into jumpers. Oh how welcome these things were in those days of such austerity.

My pocket money, which usually consisted of a three-penny bit or a silver sixpence if I was lucky, was hoarded carefully in my small woollen purse. It had to cover a lot of things – my weekly copy of *Sunny Stories*, sweets, colouring books and crayons and presents. On one occasion, I bought my mother a present. I had saved up for some time and one market day I at last accumulated enough. At the top of the town was a shop that sold china ornaments and other small gifts. I had seen a particular butter dish for some weeks, oblong, with a fitting lid. On its pale cream china sides there was a handpainted picture of a lake, trees and mysterious buildings with red roofs on the far side of the water. The picture had caught my imagination and I was determined to buy it. I think it cost about a shilling but I had saved enough and took it home wrapped in tissue paper. I gave it to my mother that evening with a carefully printed note which read, 'To dear Mummy to thank you for bringing me away from the bombs.'

On several occasions when the Reilth was full of visitors, my mother and I spent a few days here in Bishop's Castle with Mr and Mrs Robinson. We rather enjoyed the change of scene and were able to go to the Parish church nearby and wander round the little town. 'Uncle Dick' had a yard at the back of his house where building supplies were stored and the coffins were made for his undertaking business. On the floor of his shed were piles of soft sawdust and curly shavings, and propped on trestles the beautifully-made coffins with lovely ornate brass fittings, lay waiting. It was with a somewhat macabre interest that I peeped in, wondering who they were for. In one corner of the yard was an old gypsy caravan in which we were allowed to play when Gladys or Margaret called in for a cup of tea. Its ornate painted and gilded woodwork was rather faded, but inside it was fitted out with an ingenious array of cupboards and shelves. There was a small black grate and a little table. Bunk beds were neatly stowed away behind faded curtains. It was lovely to imagine living in it, drawn by a horse as one swayed along the country lanes. Mr and Mrs Robinson were very kind and owned one of the few cars in the neighbourhood. It was with them one Sunday afternoon that we discovered the exciting area known as the Stiperstones.

Chapter Twelve

WHINBERRY PICKING

Summer 1942

There is a story about the Stiperstones that was told to us as children, one of the many stories of folklore and legend which have survived in the borderlands of Shropshire. It concerned the rocks known as The Devil's Chair which dominate this rather wild stretch of country. The hills run parallel to the Long Mynd separated from it by a wonderful and little-known valley where the parishes of Pulverbatch, Wentnor and Ratlinghope lie. But on the other side, through the villages of Snailbeach and Shelve, unused mineshafts, quarries and spoil heaps litter the countryside and names like 'The Bog', 'Black Marsh', and 'Squilver' add to the mystery of this strange place. Lead was mined here from Roman times and zinc and silver have been found. But now the mines are abandoned and their derelict buildings, shafts and pits have left a desolate landscape. Above them great sweeps of heather rise to a height of some 1700 feet, where once the Corbett family were granted hunting rights and permission to take wolves, by man, dog or traps.

On the highest part of the ridge stands The Devil's Chair, its great pile dark and forbidding against the skyline, its craggy outcrop of quartzite towering over the slopes where the whinberries grow. When the mists hang low over the hill and hide the chair from view, the devil is supposed to be sitting on his throne to commune with the witches who abound in these parts; if anyone dares to sit on the chair at midnight a terrible thunderstorm will display the devil's displeasure.

On one occasion it is said he was making his way from Ireland with an apron full of stones to fill up Hell's Gutter when he sat down to rest; as he got up his apron strings broke and the stones were scattered all over the ridge where they remain to this day. Stories of ghosts abound. One is of Edric, a Saxon lord whose lands were taken from him by the Normans and who, it is said, remains a prisoner with his beautiful golden-haired wife Godda in the mines below Snailbeach. Tales are told of miners who, when working in deep shafts, have heard them knocking to be set free. Edric's spirit is thought to ride abroad on a great white horse whenever war threatens. One day Wild Edric's lands will be restored to him once more but until then, or so it is said, he takes on the form of a great black dog with fiery eyes who joins the ghosts that gather here on 22nd December each year for the Winter Solstice. Birds called the 'Seven Whistlers' too are said to haunt the Stiperstones when six birds fly up and down looking for their lost companion; and in another local tale, a phantom funeral procession can be seen at Ratlinghope.

Our minds filled with these old tales, it was with a somewhat fearful excitement that we were taken up onto the Stiperstones one Sunday afternoon in Uncle Dick's big black funeral car to pick whinberries. Luckily it was a bright sunny day and as I glanced up quickly at the huge pile of rocks, I was

Me and Mary with sheep in the yard at The Reilth

relieved to see there was no sign of mist or even a cloud in the sky, which meant there was no chance of the devil sitting there. We climbed out of the car and with bowls and baskets and a picnic tea, we spread out over the hillside. I kept close to Mary, cocking an eye skywards in case the whistlers were swooping overhead, but only the sound of skylarks echoed in the clear air, which was intoxicatingly strong and filled with the scent of heather.

Among the heather, the low-growing whinberry bushes lay, hard scratchy branches covered in small copper-coloured leaves hiding the tiny purple berries. Whinberries are very difficult to pick. The fruit is so small and so well hidden that it takes a long time to gather enough to fill even a small basket. Some people think combing them off is quicker but the number of leaves that then need to be sorted out from among the berries makes it a slow, laborious job. At first we all worked hard, bending over the low bushes, our fingers stained purple with the juice but soon the younger of us tired of the tedious task and ran off to play. Across the valley we could see the lower slopes of the Long Mynd. In the expanse of moorland the silence was only broken by our thin cries or the occasional bleating of sheep, the high liquid sound of a curlew or an occasional rook.

We ran up to the rocks, daring each other to sit on the Devil's Chair, but not quite brave enough to do so, nor to offer gifts of whinberries to the devil as some children are said to do. At last it was time for tea and we sat down rather thankfully to watch the sheep on the distant slopes and munch happily at our sandwiches. A slight wind brought a chill to the air and we

Part of the Devil's Chair on the Stiperstones where, on misty days, the Devil himself is said to sit

packed up to go. It felt safe to believe in these tales now that we were climbing once more into the soft leather seats of the car to be taken safely home. Baskets of fruit were balanced on our knees, our fingers were stained and our backs ached but it was all worth it for the whinberry pies that were to follow.

Whinberries make the most delicious pies. Mixed with a few cooking apples and topped by a crumbling crust of feather-light pastry, the result is indescribably delicious, especially with huge spoonfuls of golden cream scooped from the dishes standing in the dairy.

Another great treat was whinberry jelly, made in the same way as blackberry jelly. The fruit, apples and whinberries, cooked and strained and boiled up with some of the precious sugar, made a delicately flavoured preserve that, when spread on bread and butter, was a feast. I shall never forget the scents that filled the house while all this was being done. The smell of homemade bread as it was brought in from the brick oven in the yard, and the sight of the large golden loaves as they stood on the table. The sweet smell of the whinberries simmering gently on the range in the huge gleaming preserving pan and the sharp smell of the apples as they were sliced ready on the table.

What a comfortable atmosphere these homely tasks brought to our childhood. Sitting at the table and watching Mrs Deakins make pies and pastries and being allowed to cut out the shapes with the little metal cutter; standing in the doorway of the dairy while Mary churned the butter or stirred the huge pans of milk on the shelves; helping to pick peas in the garden, dig up the first potatoes or gather blackberries in the hedges; hanging over the cowshed door while the long row of cows stood patiently, waiting to be milked by hand; collecting eggs from the secret nests in the yard and helping to feed the hens or a cade lamb, it was a place of never-ending fascination and joy for me. We were only visitors here, yet as I sat with the other children with our backs against the ancient panels of the stairs and ate our nightly supper of bread and milk, I felt a warm security and acceptance which made me wonderfully happy to be part of this large family when all my own relations were so far away.

It must have been hard for my mother who was used to her own home and who was so much more aware of the dangers my father was in and the terrible news of the war; and yet she too loved this place, the beautiful valley, the rushing streams and rolling hills, the changing seasons on the farm with its pattern of seedtime and harvest which fascinated her. Her letters to my father were happier here but the underlying sadness of being apart was still there.

As the days of summer wore on and the hedgerows and fields began to show signs of autumn, she made her plans to go home. She was determined to be away from here before winter came and caught the valley in its icy grip once more. And so we went home, leaving the hills of Shropshire which had kept us safe, leaving the peace and tranquillity of its sequestered valleys, to face the rest of the war together with my father in our homelands in the south.

EPILOGUE

It was not until early in 1943 that we managed to find that 'little corner of our own' that my mother longed for. Strangely, it was within a mile of our former home in Pembury, Kent, but so buried away in the countryside that it felt like another world. We came to it one winter's night down a long muddy lane that seemed to sink deeper and deeper into the blackness. Unlit by moon or stars, overhung by high banks covered with thorn and trailing briars, it descended behind the church into a previously unexplored stretch of the Kentish Weald. The lane's surface was of rough uneven flints which, as we neared the bottom, became a quagmire of mud which was to remain there until well into the following spring.

About a mile off the main road, a turning to the left led past the dark silhouette of a barn up a steep bank, where our car came to rest at the gate of a cottage seen dimly through the rain in the light of our shrouded headlamps. Slipping in the thick mud we went through a small wicket gate, half blocked by the trailing branches of gooseberry bushes and the straggling remains of mint and along a brick path to the back door, past a well, which we were later to discover was our only water supply. On our left was the outhouse which held the earth closet and the washhouse, on our right under the dripping eaves, the low door of the cottage that was to be our home for over a year. The door was shut but from inside came the sound of humming, which stopped abruptly when we knocked.

As the door opened we were met by a tall figure with straggling white hair, the red cheeks of a country woman and the intensely dark eyes of a gypsy. Mrs Gare, mother of two sons, lived here at Chalkett Farm with her younger son Geoff who ran the farm. She was a somewhat fierce character who always rather scared me, but on this occasion she made us welcome enough and we went in. Inside, the kitchen which we were to share was lit by a single oil lamp, balanced on a corner of the table among a sea of objects which crowded so closely over its surface that only a small space was left uncovered. Cobwebs festooned the windows whose ledges were crammed with bottles and jars which looked as if they had been there for years. But an old black range burnt cheerfully enough and the freshly scrubbed stone flags were covered with clean sacks.

Taking our sodden coats and hurrying us through to the living room, Mrs Gare offered us a cup of tea. Again, a large fire made the shadows dance as we crowded in and looked round in vain for somewhere to sit down while space was made with difficulty for the tray of tea. Piles of newspapers filled the table and most of the chairs, old bills and letters were stuffed into the big oak desk, tins and jars filled the mantleshelf and ledges. Cold and tired after our journey, we drank the tea gratefully and waited politely for Mrs Gare to show us where we were to live.

Getting to her feet at last, she went through a small lobby with us following expectantly behind her. Here a door led into two rooms on the end of the house, one above the other and connected by their own staircase. A door into the garden came to the well and from the beautiful old windows, cracked and stuffed with newspaper to keep out the draughts, we looked out over the most beautiful view. Again a bright fire burnt in the grate and when we shut the door and were alone, it was home.

Then began one of the happiest times I can remember in my early life. We had a home and I was with my father. I even had a room of my own if I climbed a second flight of stairs to the attic and lay on a mattress on the floor, gazing out through the floor-level window at the countryside far below. I shared the attic with rows of ripening apples and kept my belongings in an old orange box covered by a piece of curtain. It held all my books and I was quite satisfied with my 'furniture'. Outside was the farm and Geoff.

Geoff was a bachelor: eccentric, quarrelsome, of strange appearance with red face and fuzzy hair and eyes as clear and alert as a wild animal's. Working single-handed on the farm, at odds with the authorities for not complying with the increasing number of regulations and caught up in endless minor court cases, still he always had time to talk to the children who came there to play and treated us all as his friends. His farming methods may have been at fault but he had a close understanding of the countryside, which he loved to share with us. Walking through the fields with his dog at his heels he would open our eyes to things of interest: the first violets, a rare bee orchid, a mallard's nest,

On the haycart at Chalkett Farm with friends

two fox cubs which he saved when their mother was killed and brought home for us to play with. He treated us with a gentle teasing humour which was never unkind and made us feel useful by giving us jobs to do for which he gave us small amounts of pocket money.

Along the top of the farmland ran the old coach road, a sandy track long supplanted by the new road. Here great beech trees grew, their twisted roots emerging from the sandy soil, their branches spreading high overhead where the wind made a sound like the sea. One, the largest, became our meeting place. Fearlessly we climbed high into the leafy bower or rode the swaying branches, pretending we were on horseback. There was always a gang of children there, Clive, Susan, Shirley, Bernar, John, Beryl, Helen and me.

Sometimes my father would join in these games. He told me stories of knights, of battles, of castles with portcullis and drawbridge. He made me bows and arrows and a rope ladder to scale the battlements of a tree we called Rollo Castle: a game which came to a sudden end when the ladder broke and left him stranded. On my eleventh birthday he made us a camp in a rough stretch of gorsey bank known as 'the Brooms'. We cooked sausages on sticks and played chasing games among the low bushes where the smell of the bare earth and the gorse made me dizzy with delight to be home again.

About this time I began to go to school again. From Chalkett Farm I went to Kent College at the far end of Pembury village. I walked, with an eye out for aircraft overhead, up our lane, through the village, down the long hill named Rolly Hill to the school which was near Pembury Old Church.

Only a few things stand out in my memory of the short time I spent there. I was proud of my uniform of butcher blue blouses and grey shorts. I enjoyed the formal lessons and the friends I made. I remember the injustice of winning a wild flower competition and having to share the prize with someone else; and being moved to a higher class where the work was more difficult and I missed my newly-made friends left behind in the form below. I remember an argument with the head mistress and feeling aggrieved that she didn't appreciate my advice.

There was a girl there who was fetched in a smart pony and trap every day and who later became a good friend – Mary Anne Berry, grand-daughter of Viscount Kemsley the newspaper baron. I played lacrosse on the lovely playing fields on Pembury Walks and sat with the lines of girls who half-filled the old Church each Sunday; but I was not really happy.

Perhaps the contrast to my one-to-one tuition with my mother and my freedom on the farm was too much to cope with; but it was not until later when, at the age of twelve, I started at a school in Tunbridge Wells that I settled down and began, for the first time in my life, to learn French and Latin, geometry and algebra, and thought it was all wonderful. In spite of the war which still formed the background to our lives, I think my parents were extremely happy to be together again and to have the semblance of a home once more. My father went off to work in Tunbridge Wells on 'Jimmy', his moped, and

In the autumn of 1940, as the war-clouds gathered, I was always outside in the fields, helping with the harvest

came home each night to a warm fire and a meal with his family. My mother had not only the joy of being back with my father, her family and friends, but also the farm life in which she took such an interest. Our own furniture was still in store and the conditions were far from ideal; an outside lavatory consisting of a wooden seat and a pit, no bathroom or running water, the shared cramped kitchen, unheated bedrooms and oil lamps in an old neglected house which, genuine Tudor, was both draughty and damp. Yet my mother had an amazing capacity to override these things if she was well and happy, and an ability to see through the roughest of exteriors to the gentle character beneath.

I was in paradise. I talked to Geoff endlessly, following him everywhere as he went about the old farm buildings which had not changed much over the years. Nor had the rutted tracks leading out to the fields. Tall hedges and scrubby banks held secret paths and hidden dens where I spent hours in imaginative games, often quite alone among the leafy branches. There were woods where the ground was yellow with primroses, or white with anemones or blue with the massed heads of bluebells which lapped among the tree roots like a vast azure sea. Here were badger setts and foxholes and the musty scent of stoat, which clung to the damp moss under the beeches. Birds nested undisturbed in the thick undergrowth and filled the woodland with their calls.

In the far corner of the wood was an encampment of Romany gypsies; their wooden caravans drawn up round a fire. They were a secret people who rarely spoke to us except to sell their little hazel twig baskets of primroses, clothes pegs or bunches of heather. Geoff seemed to have an understanding with them and they never troubled us although I was told not to go near their encampment. Behind the house was the old orchard where plum, cherry and apple trees stood in straggling rows of creamy wonder in spring and the glowing abundance of fruit in summer. I was allowed to climb the tall ladder and pick the fruit, and laid it carefully in a bucket lined with leaves. From here I could see down through the swaying boughs to where the cows waited to be called in for milking, or see the pigs in their sty, or Mrs Gare in her garden picking beans. In a field beyond the orchard was a place where two large, cup-shaped hollows sloped towards the south and caught the sun. Deep enough to be protected from the wind, their sides too steep for cattle to negotiate, they were untouched and uncultivated, making a perfect haven for wildlife. A single oak tree hung over the grassy banks. Primroses, violets, harebells and celandines grew there undisturbed. The air was full of the sound of insects, butterflies and bees.

Surrounded by willow and alder there was a pond where in the damp soil rushes grew intermingled with ladies' smock and kingcups. Moorhens, silent and secretive, lurked among the stems by the water, frogs spawned in the shallows and a pair of mallards paraded their young. On the banks birds hid in the thorn thickets or among the branches of yellow palm, while dragonflies flew swiftly to and fro and water boatmen made their haphazard way over the surface of the silky water. I came here almost daily, enthralled by its loveliness. I lay on the grass breathing in its warm scents, my fingers clutching at the earth's gritty substance. I gazed up

Haymaking at Chalkett Farm, Pembury, 1944

111

through the green stems into the blue vastness above me and revelled in my freedom. Crunching apples picked up from the abundance of windfalls on my way through the orchard, happy in the knowledge of my reunited family, I lay lost in daydreams, alert to the small sounds around me and the skylarks singing as they rose high overhead into the blue infinity that I knew held God. These were moments of pure happiness, the kind of moments which are searched for the rest of our lives when childhood is gone and they are lost among the debris that life scatters round us in the passing of the years.

And it was debris indeed that was scattered around us night after night. Pembury and its surrounding district was right in the path of enemy aircraft as they approached London, and every effort was made to stop the planes reaching that city with their death-dealing loads. The opposition was heavy and many planes were brought down over the Kentish countryside or turned for home, dropping their bombs before they fled. Incendiary bombs fell in large numbers and our fire fighters were busy putting out the flames.

People like my father had a brief training which consisted, among other things, of being shut in a shed full of burning straw with a bucket of water and a stirrup pump. At night when he was on duty he wore a tin hat which was supposed to protect him from shrapnel, which fell over the village, littering our gardens, so that in the morning it was possible to pick it up, often still warm. Sometimes we found brass shell cases which people polished and kept on their mantelpiece as a kind of souvenir.

It was in 1944 that we had the luck to hear of a furnished house to let in Lower Green Road, Pembury, right in the centre of the village and just below the village green. It was here that we were to spend the rest of the war. 'Ravilious', so-named after the artist who was a relative of the owner, was a three bedroomed house built between the wars of solid red brick and white woodwork. It was a cheerful-looking house with a garden back and front, and looked over the extensive playing fields known as 'The Rec'. Inside, it was typical of many houses of that period, sparsely furnished and plainly decorated with no extra luxuries, but it was a home at last.

Next-door on one side were a family of Hungarian refugees, whose pretty dark-eyed daughter tried to speak to me in English but who had a sad air about her, only occasionally broken by a smile when my father gently teased her. On the other side lived two maiden ladies, retired teachers with whom my mother became friendly. With a house to ourselves we began to pick up the threads of our lives that had been shattered by our long separation. My parents were very sociable and friends frequently called in to tea or to share a musical evening. My father became organist of a local church and both my mother and I joined the choir. He was also a member of the local dramatic society and there were many hilarious evenings of rehearsals in our front room.

My attempts at drama were rather less welcome. The house was always full of children and on one occasion we decided to act out a woodland scene in the dining room. This entailed bringing in large branches with which we proceeded to make the required woodland setting. My mother came home to find the room crammed with ceiling-height branches and the floor covered in a thick layer of leaves. She complained rather feebly about the mess but on being told it was all quite necessary for the play, she gave in. She was always very tolerant of things we did.

Another of our games was a rather wild one on horseback entailing 'capturing prisoners' from the 'enemy' camp, which meant a great deal of tearing up and down the sandy tracks of a forested area behind the village. Several of my friends had ponies, good-natured animals who did not object when we tried out various circus acts on their broad backs.

But there was one place in the house that was my secret. The small box-room above the front door was full of the owner's possessions and was kept locked. Somehow I discovered that I could open the door and crawl to the far end where, behind the mounds of furniture and cases, was a space, just big enough for me to lie in, by a large bookcase full of the books which had belonged to the two boys who had lived there. They were books of adventure, of discovery and exploration and old copies of the 'Boy's Own Paper'. Many had the names of the two boys on the fly sheet, Don and Peter, and in the front of one there were a few loose photographs which, dim and crumpled as they were, showed two boys with remarkable good looks, one tall dark and serious, and the other smiling, with the fair good looks of a young film star. I gazed at them with curiosity and with a feeling of sadness and disbelief for I knew that both boys had joined the Air Force and that Peter, the fair one, had become a fighter pilot who was shot down and killed just before his 21st birthday. Don his brother was still in the Air Force as a navigator on one of the big bombers, a Lancaster I believe, and would come to the house sometimes, a tall rather sombre figure in uniform who was later to become a great family friend. It was many years later that I found among his belongings a letter from his father telling him of his brother Peter's death and enclosing a photograph of that beautiful young man *(see Appendix)*.

The conflict was at its height. There were the worst shipping losses of the war and the shortages that resulted were worse than ever. But there were also the first signs of hope.

Rommel was retreating in North Africa and after the victory at El Alamein the bells were rung from Westminster Abbey and Coventry's one surviving bell tower. Hitler gave the order for retreat after failures in Stalingrad and Leningrad. In 1942 the Allied Forces had begun to advance and Churchill saw it as the beginning of a change in our favour. He called for unity saying, 'The whole future of mankind may depend on our actions and on our conduct'. On 3rd September 1943, Italy was invaded. But things were not over yet. A 'little blitz' hit London and the Allies retaliated with fearsome raids over Hamburg, Berlin and Nuremburg, where the chance of survival for our aircrews was said to be 50/50. In June there were massive infantry landings in Normandy and everyone felt things were on the move. The Germans failed to stop the advance and France was liberated.

But the fight at home still went on. We became used to the sight of barrage balloons floating in the sky above us and the sound of the siren which, night after night, would get us up out of our warm beds as we heard the roar of enemy planes overhead and the crash of guns and bombs. My father was often out on A.R.P. duty and so my mother and I would sit alone, crouched in the cupboard under the stairs which, in the absence of a shelter, was considered to be the safest place in the house. Holding a pillow ready to put over our heads in an emergency, my mother would pass the time by reading aloud. Her favourite was the 91st Psalm, *'Thou shalt not be afraid for the terror by night, nor for the arrow that flieth by day; nor for the pestilence that walketh in darkness, nor for the destruction that wasteth at noonday.'* It seemed appropriate.

On one occasion my father charged in the back door yelling 'Look out!' He had heard the warning sounds of a bomber very close and we sat rigid as a string of bombs was dropped right across the village, just missing our house and landing in the graveyard and in the fields of Downingbury Farm where my father had stayed while we were away. The following day there were stories of the chaos in the graveyard. We went to see the crater in the field which was 'big enough to hold a double decker bus'.

It was after this narrow escape that we decided to share a shelter with Miss Martin and Miss Usher, next door. Properly made of concrete with steps leading to an underground chamber, we were told it would give protection against anything but a direct hit. When the siren sounded we would leave our warm beds and, with blankets and pillows, creep down the dark garden lit only by the probing searchlights overhead and into this hole in the ground. Here we would find the two ladies with a welcome thermos of tea. Miss Martin would usually be wearing two hats, which for some reason known only to her, she felt would protect her from the bombs. I don't think we slept much. The walls smelt strongly of damp concrete and were very cold to the touch. We would sit, huddled on a narrow camp bed, listening to the sounds of aircraft overhead and wait for the all-clear to tell us it was safe to go back to bed. The only other sound was the regular click as cockroaches fell down the steps. When they reached the bottom we would take it in turns to throw them back into the garden.

At weekends we often went to visit my grandparents in Lewes. In fact the first few months after our return from Shropshire was spent with them while I attended a small school nearby. Everything was just as I remembered. It was like a rock in the changing patterns of my life. Seeing again my grandmother's beautiful, serene smile as she held out her arms to me, it was as though I had never been away. My bedroom was still there over the porch with the patch in the wallpaper where I, with my three-year-old fingers, had carefully torn a path among the flowers on the newly-decorated wall. The view of the Downs from the window beyond the dark garden; the smell of the apples in the shed and the geraniums in the conservatory; apple pies, fruit cake and cucumber sandwiches for tea; all was as it had been before. It was inconceivable that it could ever have been overrun by the trampling feet of enemy armies, our dear folk lost and frightened, perhaps never to be seen again. It was the one place I felt would always be there.

It was when the 'doodlebugs' started in the June of 1944 that we used the shelter most. These were flying bombs, unmanned explosives which were yet another attempt to cause terror among the civilian population. London emptied under their attack more than in 1940. Deep shelters were now being used. Many thousands of mothers and children were once more said to be leaving. 'Bomb alley' across Kent and Sussex suffered particularly heavily. 200,000 houses were destroyed or damaged. The 'Flying bombs', or V1s, were fired from sites on the French coast and came over with almost clock-like regularity. We could often time the exact moment when it was best to go to the shelter while they passed over. It was quite usual for my mother to have to leave off cooking my father's breakfast several times and rush into the shelter. We would hear the distinctive sound of their approach and listen for them to pass over safely, their fat tube-like shape with its small fins, disappearing in the direction of London. It was when the sound of the engine stopped that we were worried, as this meant it was coming down somewhere nearby. Sometimes we would see one go over safely and would relax until one of the fast flying fighters in hot pursuit would manage to tip its wing and it would be turned round only to totter unsteadily back over our heads once more, sinking gradually lower until it hit the ground with a loud explosion; one at least which had not reached the crowded city streets where it could do so much more harm.

After the flying bombs came the rockets. These I found much more frightening, as they would land with a terrific roar with no warning, which I found very unnerving. They contained one ton of explosive. One landed close to our school in Tunbridge Wells and I remember feeling very afraid for days afterwards. One landed on Woolworth's in New Cross and killed 160 people. But the days went by and life went on.

After two attempts at home tuition, I was by now attending a school in Tunbridge Wells, which I loved. I went in each day with my pony-riding friends, Mary Anne Berry and Betty Insoll. I was in the school netball team, had tennis coaching, and would one day become house and gymnastics captain, a prefect and head girl. It was all a far cry from my days on a farm in the Shropshire hills, but with its novelty value to inspire me, and the security of its rather rigid routine, I loved it.

Eventually on 4th May 1945, the German forces surrendered and 8th May was declared V.E. day. The war in Europe came to an end and our life began to return to normal. Of course the war with Japan was still raging and it was not until after the atom bombs of Hiroshima and Nagasaki in August that Japan surrendered and the world war was truly over. The aftermath was terrible as people counted the cost and began to repair the damage but at least we were at peace. My life was crowded with many things in the coming years, but one day in the far distant future, the call of the Welsh borderlands was so strong that I returned there to settle with my husband in a village not so far from Mainstone, and within sight of those glorious Shropshire hills.

Appendix

A letter to our friend Don, written by his father to tell him of his brother Peter's death:

Pembury. 25 November 1941

Dear Don,

Can you brace yourself for what's to come? I have hesitated about sending this wondering how far you had recovered from your groggy turn. Your thoughts and mine, Don, have never been far from the lad in the East, and sometimes a grim shudder came over us. On Saturday last, Don, I had a fateful visitor, a telegram. Bear up old chap, it was the worst. Dear old Pete is no more, in the enclosed envelope you'd find the confirmatory letter of the sad news.

Peter, the fighter pilot killed before his 21st birthday

    In the face of this hard blow, Don, try with all that's in you to feel of Peter that he passed in his clean and sweet youth, spared everything of thought and agony and spared above all of lying, a broken wreck, possibly blind for years in hospital, where are many such alas poor lads, this would have been harrow indeed for us; what has happened in time we can steel ourselves to bear, and try to think of others less stoutly built who feel hopelessly crushed at their loss. There is this grand comfort, Don. You've been as good a brother to Pete as life holds; I've tried with all that's in me to be a good and kindly father. We have nothing to reproach ourselves with. And you've given a loved brother, and I a dear son, to England; those are deathless thoughts. We shall have the deep respect of our fellow citizens.

There is something brighter in store lad for us somewhere, someday. I have faith still left for that. When I think of my dark 1932 days, when at Chartham, and all hope had left me, and then that marvellous deliverance and a God-sent recovery and rehabilitation I feel that the sunlight is for you and me yet. If you anyhow can, Don, get out of the air and on a ground job, with all that's in me I urge you to do this: the dread of you in the planes again is a nightmare. I think you could be granted compassionate leave, it used to be given even in the Great War when possible.

In conclusion Don lad, hold to this as an impregnable fortress. You have still a loved sister and brother and a darling little one at Peterborough; there's dear old Auntie yet, and a very rock, immovable, clean, steady and resolute in Dad. We're an iron wall behind you, Don. Carry this letter with you, read it often, it will give you solace and be a girder.

God bless you Don.

Dad

PS. We're at Calvary Rd if you are coming.

A letter to my father from his mother:
Heathfields, Hamsey Road, Barcombe, Sussex
30 March 1941

My dear Leslie,
Thought I would write a line to you to let you know we are alright and hope you are safe and well and that you have had a nice weekend with G and not had any scares. We have had about 11 warnings this week, 3 on one day and 4 the other two days but not very long ones. I expect we shall soon be having something now they have had one or two set backs, but we do not get very much here thank goodness and not much traffic at present, in Lewes they have those great tanks and the noise is terrible.

When you phone Uncle Harry tell him to take his registration card with him if he goes to Lewes, they stop you before you get to the barrier and soldiers and policemen to look at them also this side or the Chalk Field they stop all the traffic etc. What a game! I hope I shall have a letter from you soon to know if you are coming down this weekend. If I were you I should get your address altered then if Dorothy does come back to Glengariff you would be alright. I don't know if they are stopping traffic anywhere else and I cannot find out at present.

I have heard from Dorothy yesterday. They seem much better, also a photo of Anthea. Anthea wrote a note to Dad and myself on one half sheet. She was very pleased with the little bag of biscuits and hankies I sent her, not the one you saw, one I have had ever since May. I sent the one you saw as well. We have been to church this morning, very keen wind today, have not stirred far this afternoon. Dad is having a tune up. Auntie Mab says they have been very quiet in Merton for a few nights. It is very bright tonight. I hope they will stay at home. Now I must close, with fond love from us both Trusting you are keeping well.

Your loving Mum and Dad

Heathfields, Hamsey Road, Barcombe.
9 April 1941

My dear Leslie,
Thought I would write a few lines before you go on Saturday to see D. and A. Will you kindly drop me a P.C. as soon as you get there to say if you arrive safely and if D. and A. are safe and well as we hear the Rats went to Coventry last night and I think it is not far from them.

We had a dreadful night last night, been a bit quieter today also this evening although there were three [bombs] dropped about an hour ago. Last night it began about 7 in the evening and kept on the whole night and we heard them until 7 this morning. They seem to have had it very bad in Brighton and Shoreham. We heard the bombs drop and on Monday night late we heard 6 go, it is fairly quiet now but do not know how long it will last.

We do hope you are safe and well and that you will have a safe journey there and back but do let me know if you arrive safely and get back home safe. Hope it will be fine and that you will all have a good time, we are fairly well only feel a bit tired after last night. No one seems to have had any sleep this way but if it still keeps quiet we shall soon go upstairs. So now I must close trusting everything will be alright. With kind love from us both to you all

Yours always,
Mum and Dad

P.S. Thank you very much for your letter this morning. I am sorry to see by the paper they have been round Warwickshire so do let me have a P.C. to know if they are safe when you get there. I really think they would be as safe here as there, you do not seem safe anywhere now and I think they would be better with their own folk, but of course you know best.

Letter from my father to my mother from Uncle Harry's house in Buxted, Sussex [his pet-name for her was Tom].

Four Oaks, Buxted.

My darling Tom,

As I believe I told you I am here for the weekend. Came yesterday but was rather late arriving as I had a massage from Mrs Malden in the afternoon and then just as I was at the farm collecting my bag Frank Roberts came in with his thumb badly cut and I took him to hospital and waited while he had two stitches in and brought him back. Then I had a puncture on the way over! So I arrived about 5pm and Uncle was beginning to wonder where I was.

You asked in a previous letter if Buxted is a quiet place to come to. As far as I have seen this weekend it is NOT the place!! It seems to have a far worse time than Lewes and even Pembury. Last week was quieter than the few hours I have been here. Last night as we were sitting here the whole place suddenly shook and 4 bombs came down not very far away. During the evening we counted 12 altogether, more or less near.

There were 4 more in the night and then this morning about 12.00 some planes were overhead and suddenly there was a TERRIFIC rattle. I thought it was a car crashing on the road and was just going out to see when the front door (where I was) nearly came in 4 times and there were 4 hefty bangs. Uncle and Uncle Jack were in the garden and they scuttled in like rabbits. They dropped just up the road. We could see the smoke. Now there is one long drone overhead and we sit just waiting and wondering if and when and where any will drop.

So you see Buxted is NOT a place I can recommend you to come to!! Uncle says it is always more or less like this. I have wondered sometimes, when he had said on the phone that he'd been very disturbed, if he was exaggerating but I can see now that he was definitely not!! We were just changing the wheel on the car this morning when my aunt and uncle from Wimbledon arrived unexpectedly. I was very pleased to see them and thought that although rather worn they seem to be standing the strain very well. They have not had their clothes off (except for a hurried bath) in 8 weeks! Aunt sleeps on a couch in the corner of the dining room protected by a table and Uncle Jack sleeps in a chair. They have a shelter but find it so,'tomb-like' that they prefer to risk it at home.

They had some dreadful tales and it is obvious from what they said that we know literally nothing from the papers of what is going on. They say the destruction around them there is very bad indeed.

I am afraid I have no more news of myself. I had this heat and massage yesterday to help me. I felt fine at the time but the effect soon wears off. And today I am about the same. My uncle Jack if you remember has had the same kind of trouble for a long time and he agrees with me that the heat and massage only relieve for a time. We found we had many pains in common!!

The garden here is now rather bare. It has been very pretty indeed all through the summer. I wish you could have seen it. Perhaps you will next summer, who knows? Like you I am getting tired of this existence and only wish we could all be together again, wherever it might be. I should be content with the simplest things. Your mother estimated that my tastes are so plain that I can be kept for 10/6d a week.

Personally, when we do start again I should like life to be a little less complicated than it was so that we have more time for each other and don't go to bed so worn out that all we can do is lie like logs and go to sleep and wake up tired. Shall we see what we can do about it? I am enclosing a short letter to Anthea. How I long to see that child again. You can't imagine how I miss her. I have not found anything out about H.H. yet. I am sorry she is not liking school. I am rather worried about her education. I am afraid it will suffer. What do you think about a boarding school in a safe area? Look after yourself, my pet. I am longing to see you.

All my love, John

Articles from the *Kent and Sussex Courier* (1941)
The town mentioned was Tunbridge Wells.

NIGHT ATTACK OVER SOUTH-EAST ENGLAND

Showers of incendiaries over a wide area. Fourteen German bombers out of an estimated total of 90 were destroyed in the course of raids over South East England during Friday night. From the moment they crossed the coastline and attempted to reach London they had to face intense gunfire. Searchlights picked out the enemy planes and many fierce aerial battles were fought over Kentish towns and villages. In one area the raiders dropped flares that lit up a wide expanse of countryside while those below heard machine-gun bursts and many saw at least three of the raiders brought down. Two were on fire and diving to destruction; another was seen to explode in the air after one of our night fighters got in a couple of short bursts of cannon fire. In the heat of the battle several of the bombers released their loads haphazardly.

It was when a night fighter got within combat range that one of the enemy released his compliment of incendiaries over a town. But the Civil Defence Services were on the alert and incidents were quickly dealt with while no serious damage or casualties were reported. In one part of the town where there were ancient buildings a fire bomb landed in the rafters of what is now a furniture store.

Mr S.A. Gardener, who was fire-watching was busy with bombs in the street outside, when he saw a glow from the roof. He rushed inside and found that the bomb had landed in the one part of the roof that could be got at above the lift shaft. It was soon put out.

A shock awaited the sons of Mr and Mrs Cook when they found an incendiary in their bed. Fortunately they were not in bed at the time. In this area fire bombs fell everywhere. One public house had a narrow escape from three bombs. Two sergeants of the R.A. did some magnificent work in helping the Civil Defence forces.

NURSE'S BRAVERY

Another part of the town also had its quota of incendiaries. In the private hotel, where the proprietress' mother had been lying bedridden for five months, a bomb landed in her bedroom. Flames barred the way of escape, but her nurse rushed into the room and carried her out through the burning door. 'The wardens and firefighters were soon on the job, and everything was under control in a very short while,' said the owner.

Another hotel received four bombs. A woman and child had come down from their own bedroom to that of their maid, and the bomb landed beside the bed. They managed to escape. Another, high up in the window coping of another bedroom, burnt itself out. Seven incendiaries dropped in the courtyard between this building and the one next-door, three falling on the roof of a large block of flats just behind. One bomb fell on a hut in the grounds of a Civil Defence headquarters, where a girl was sleeping. Many dropped on waste ground and some houses suffered superficial damage. Everywhere one comment was to the fore; 'The fire-fighting and Civil Defence services did magnificent work- they were all on their toes.' This was the first real test since the battle of Britain.

A BLAZING TRAIL

In a neighbourhood well known to hop-pickers one bomber was brought down in flames. Previously a basket of incendiaries had been released over the surrounding area. The plane appeared to explode, strewing wreckage all over the locality. It was still blazing when the police and National Fire Service arrived on the scene. They found the main section of the fuselage, partially submerged in a small pond by the main road, around which was burning oil. Rescuers were unable to get very close owing to the intense heat. One German was found dead nearby, and another in the pond. There appeared to be only one survivor of the crew; he was found injured in a nearby orchard and was removed to hospital. Although the fuselage of the machine had fallen in the adjoining copse, the nose and engine became embedded in the ground not six yards away from the hotel, the walls of which were pitted with shrapnel, while the windows of the public bar had been blown out. The garden claimed a torn tyre, many pieces of unrecognisable metal, and two maps, found in the chicken run. The only casualty at the hotel itself was 'Whisky' a cat, who is now minus a part of his left ear. Mr and Mrs Older said they had been awake some time listening to the planes, when they heard machine-gun fire overhead, followed by a deafening screech, like the roar of an oncoming express train. 'I saw a huge flash of flame by the window,' said Mr Older, 'and then an impact threw me out of bed.' He and his wife and daughter immediately got up, and found numerous small fires from the burning wreckage strewn all around.

Acknowledgments

Firstly, I should like to thank my publishers Merlin Unwin Books for the help and enthusiasm which they showed all the way through the preparation of *Beneath Safer Skies*. Their guidance and support made the publishing experience a pleasure and delight and gave me faith in my own work. They became my friends.

I should like to say thank you to my daughter-in-law Patricia for her invaluable help in sorting out my endless computer problems. Also to Nic.

Also my cousin Robin who was there and shares so many memories. He was tireless in his meticulous correction of the text, for which I was very grateful.

And of course my husband Tim for his suggestions, endless patience and unwavering support, backing me up with food and drink when needed, and providing a calming voice in times of stress.

I remember with gratitude all the members of the Deakins family who welcomed me into their home and made my stay in Mainstone so interesting and such fun.

Working on this story has brought back memories of my parents who sacrificed a great deal to keep me safe and to whom I owe so much. They were very special people.

Also published by Merlin Unwin Books

A Shropshire Lad A. E. Housman

Nearest Earthly Place to Paradise
The Literary Landscape of Shropshire
Margaret Wilson and Geoff Taylor

Behind Closed Doors *in an English Country Town*
Pauline Fisk

The Temptation and Downfall of the Vicar of Stanton Lacy
Peter Klien

A Most Rare Vision *Shropshire from the Air* Mark Sisson

It Happened in Shropshire Bob Burrows

A View from the Tractor Roger Evans

A Farmer's Lot Roger Evans

Living off the Land Frances Mountford

My Animals and Other Family Phyllida Barstow

A Job for all Seasons *My Small Country Living*
Phyllida Barstow

Exraordinary Villages Tony Francis

A Beekeeper's Progress John Phipps

For more details see: www.merlinunwin.co.uk